# The Resistible Rise of Benito Mussolini

## Tom Behan

BOOKMARKS

**London and Sydney**

**The Resistible Rise of Benito Mussolini – Tom Behan**
First published 2003
Bookmarks Publications Ltd, c/o 1 Bloomsbury Street, London WC1B 3QE,
England
Bookmarks, PO Box A338, Sydney South, NSW 2000, Australia
Copyright © Bookmarks Publications Ltd

ISBN 1 898876 90 8
Printed by Bath Press
Cover by Laurence Cliffe

**Bookmarks Publications Ltd is linked to an international grouping of
socialist organisations:**

- **Australia:** International Socialist Organisation, PO Box A338, Sydney
  South. *iso@iso.org.au*
- **Austria:** Linkswende, Postfach 87, 1108 Wien. *linkswende@yahoo.com*
- **Britain:** Socialist Workers Party, PO Box 82, London E3 3LH.
  *enquiries@swp.org.uk*
- **Canada:** International Socialists, PO Box 339, Station E, Toronto, Ontario
  M6H 4E3. *iscanada@on.aibn.com*
- **Cyprus:** Ergatiki Demokratia, PO Box 27280, Nicosia.
  *wd@workersdemocracy.net*
- **Czech Republic:** Socialisticka Solidarita, PO Box 1002, 11121 Praha 1.
  *socsol@email.cz*
- **Denmark:** Internationale Socialister, PO Box 5113, 8100 Aarhus C.
  *intsoc@socialister.dk*
- **Finland:** Sosialistiliitto, PL 288, 00171 Helsinki. *info@sosialistiliitto.org*
- **France:** Socialisme par en bas, BP 15-94111, Arcueil Cedex. *speb@mageos.com*
- **Germany:** Linksruck, Postfach 304 183, 20359 Hamburg. *info@linksruck.de*
- **Ghana:** International Socialist Organisation, PO Box TF202, Trade Fair,
  Labadi, Accra
- **Greece:** Sosialistiko Ergatiko Komma, c/o Workers Solidarity, PO Box 8161,
  Athens 100 10. *sek@otenet.gr*
- **Holland:** Internationale Socialisten, PO Box 92025, 1090AA Amsterdam.
  *info@internationalesocialisten.org*
- **Ireland:** Socialist Workers Party, PO Box 1648, Dublin 8. *swp@clubi.ie*
- **Italy:** Comunismo dal Basso, Leeder, CP Bologna, Succ 5. *dalbasso@hotmail.com*
- **New Zealand:** Socialist Workers Organisation, PO Box 13-685, Auckland.
  *socialist-worker@pl.net*
- **Norway:** Internasjonale Socialisterr, Postboks 9226, Grønland, 0134 Oslo.
  *sarbeide@online.no*
- **Poland:** Pracownicza Demokracja, PO Box 12, 01-900 Warszawa 118.
  *pracdem@go2.pl*
- **Spain:** En Lucha, Apartado 563, 08080 Barcelona. *enlucha@hotmail.com*
- **United States:** Left Turn, PO Box 445, New York, NY 10159-0445.
  *left-turn@left-turn.org*
- **Uruguay:** Izquierda Revolucionaria. *ir@adinet.com.uy*
- **Zimbabwe:** International Socialist Organisation, PO Box 6758, Harare.
  *isozim@hotmail.com*

# The Resistible Rise of Benito Mussolini

# Contents

# Acknowledgements

This book owes an enormous intellectual and practical debt to Eros Francescangeli. Other than that, Toby Abse, Chris Bambery, Ian Birchall and Barbara Rampoldi all made useful comments on an earlier draft, while Emma Bircham and Dave Waller made the production process look very easy.

## About the author

Tom Behan is a longstanding member of the Socialist Workers Party, and author of *See Naples and Die* and *Dario Fo: Revolutionary Theatre*. He teaches Italian at the University of Kent at Canterbury.

## Cover pictures

The background to the picture of Mussolini on the front cover shows the names of those known to have fought on the barricades in Parma in 1922, while the back cover picture is of a barricade in Parma.

# Chronology

1860  Unification of Italy.

1892  Italian Socialist Party (PSI) formed.

1904  First general strike, mainly led by revolutionary syndicalists.

1906  Foundation of 'official' trade union confederation, CGL.

1914  June: 'Red Week' of insurrections.

1915  May: Italy enters the First World War after months of polarised arguments.

1919  March: Fascist movement founded.
      July: Two-day general strike in support of Soviet Russia.
      November: PSI becomes largest party in parliament.

1920  September: Occupation of the factories.
      November: Fascist attack on PSI-controlled Bologna council kills 10.

1921  January: Italian Communist Party (PCI) formed.
      May: In last fully democratic election, fascists gain 35 out of over 500 seats.
      June: *Arditi del popolo* (ADP) created.
      July: First and last ADP national congress and march. Successful anti-fascist resistance in Sarzana leaves 18 fascists dead.
      August: As part of 'peace pact', PSI disowns the *Arditi del popolo*.
      November: Fascists suffer five dead in a failed 'first' March on Rome.

1922  August: Failure of 'legalitarian' national general strike.
      August: Successful general strike and anti-fascist resistance in Parma.
      October: Mussolini becomes prime minister after second March on Rome.

1945  Mussolini executed by anti-fascist partisans.

# Northern Italy

# Introduction

As soon as news of the fascists' arrival spread, the local leadership of the *Arditi del popolo* called a meeting with squad leaders straight away, and gave them instructions to immediately build barricades, trenches, and barbed wire defences, using any material available. At dawn, when the order was given to get the guns out and launch the insurrection, working-class people took to the streets – as bold as the waters of a river which is bursting its banks... Men, women, old people, young people from all parties and from no party at all were all there, united in a single iron will – resist and fight...

In the early hours of day six we were informed from reliable sources that the fascist leadership had decided to launch a major attack... At seven the following morning our observers noticed columns moving from one point on the outskirts to another in a confused and disorderly fashion... The fascists, who were by this stage no longer in military formation, were roaming about in all directions in a great rush – with no command structure – jumping onto trains that were leaving, onto lorries, bicycles, or on foot. This wasn't a retreat, but the scattering of large groups of men who clambered aboard any means of transport they found, or who ran through the streets, or into the countryside, as if they were frightened of being chased.[1]

This quote, from Parma in August 1922, describes the beginning and conclusion of a triumphant act of mass resistance against the biggest force of fascist squads ever launched against a working-class community. It was one of many victories scored against the fascists in this period, led by an organisation that is at the heart of this book – the *Arditi del popolo*.[2]

In September 1920 Italy was on the verge of a socialist revolution.

Just over two years later Benito Mussolini's fascists took power and ushered in an era of severe repression, war and genocide.

The reasons behind this extraordinary turnaround are described in the following chapters, but the crucial question is, was the rise of fascism inevitable, or was another world possible in Italy 80 years ago?

The organisation that forms the central part of this book, the *Arditi del popolo* (ADP), was the first anti-fascist movement in the world. Although its existence was brief, its success was astonishing. Just a few weeks after the birth of a national organisation in June 1921, local ADP groups were able to inflict significant defeats on organised fascist groups and stem the growing menace of violent attacks against working-class organisations. The successful defence of towns such as Sarzana caused widespread disquiet within the fascist movement, almost leading to a split.

Despite this initial success, the ADP faced massive opposition from political forces that were also on the receiving end of fascist attacks. Ivanoe Bonomi's government – one of Italy's last democratic governments before Mussolini's dictatorship – actively opposed the *Arditi*, framing its leaders and unleashing widespread police repression.

But it was the hostility of the organised left that sealed the fate of the ADP. Although the ADP were committed to defending working-class communities, the leadership of both the newly formed Communist Party (PCI) and the Socialist Party (PSI) officially refused to work with the group. This led to the ADP's political isolation and disorientation. And despite further heroic and successful resistance – such as the battle of Parma described above – the ADP and the left in general were unable to stop Mussolini taking power in October 1922 and unleashing a wave of repression.

Despite the initial success of the ADP, the group has been largely erased from history. The fact that the first book on the ADP was only published in Italy in 1994 owes much to the hostility of left-wing parties at the time, and their subsequent failure to face up to their own fatal mistakes. The historiography of the working class has been dominated by Communist and Socialist historians, and it was these organisations that were unwilling to recognise some uncomfortable truths. As one writer commented:

> The *Arditi del popolo* movement lasted only a short period, due to the harsh repression meted out by the state, and the fact that the left-wing and democratic forces didn't support it as they ought to have done. Instead, almost immediately, they sabotaged and betrayed it.
>
> The movement was a real 'fleeting moment' for democratic forces, and if the challenge had been taken up they could have blocked fascism's road to power and avoided the experience of a dictatorship which lasted for over 20 years.[3]

The lessons that emerge from this story for anti-fascists and the left today are twofold: (1) the need to avoid placing ideological purity before involvement in anti-fascist struggle; and (2) to place no faith in parliament or the police stopping the rise of fascism. While these principles remain hugely relevant in the struggle against fascism today, the story of the ADP also represents a far more positive and tantalising notion – that Italian fascism could have been prevented.

The consequences of stopping fascism in Italy would have been tremendous. Without Mussolini's victory the forces of out-right reaction, and names such as Hitler and Himmler, might have never become known, and the town of Auschwitz might never have become a byword for barbarism. During his long rise to power Adolf Hitler made no secret of his admiration for *il duce* in Rome. Indeed, when Hitler first met Mussolini he asked him for his autograph.

Similarly, the defeat of fascism in Italy could have had some influence on the fate of the Russian Revolution and the wave of mass working-class struggles that engulfed Europe in the years after the First World War. A victory for anti-fascists in Italy would have led to a huge increase in the strength and confidence of the left, and perhaps even to further revolutionary bids for power.

This story is also relevant today because it shows the need

for joint political work in order to defeat a common enemy – something that became known as the united front almost at the same time as Mussolini took power. Whether it be stopping scabbing during a strike, campaigning against a war or fighting the fascists, what constantly emerges in the history of the left is the need for unity in action.

All of this matters in Italy too, as the political descendants of Mussolini, *Alleanza Nazionale* (National Alliance, or NA), are currently in government. From the moment they entered office, the NA's leaders have attempted to wipe out any commemoration of anti-fascism both during the Second World War and during Mussolini's rise to power after the First World War. Furthermore, there is a concerted attempt to commemorate on equal terms anti-fascist partisans and fascist soldiers who died in the Italian civil war of 1943-45. But they have also gone further – for example, the NA mayor of Ragusa in Sicily tried to get a seven metre high bronze statue of a fascist leader who had been a minister in Mussolini's government erected in his local town.

Many NA politicians are still completely unrepentant about the fascist dictatorship that ruled the country for 20 years. For example, in April 2001 Benito Mussolini's grandson, Guido, was campaigning to become mayor of Rome, and said: 'Mussolini's ideas were 99 percent good and 1 percent questionable.'

Outside Italy, fascism remains a significant force in France, and in Britain the fascist British National Party has recently gained a toehold with the election of three councillors in Burnley.

Therefore the story of the ADP is not just a historical curiosity in a faraway land – its experience provides us with arguments and inspiration that are still much needed. The mistakes made by the Italian left in this period, as well as the positive achievements of the ADP, need to be understood and used as part of the struggle against neo-fascism today.

# A place called Italy

Two main factors help in identifying the seeds from which Italian fascism grew, and also help in understanding the traditions of the Italian left.

Firstly, the birth of the nation-state happened much later in Italy than other European countries – in 1860 – and did not occur due to widespread popular support. Despite claims that Italy was united by a 'plebiscite', only 2 percent of the population were able to vote – 98 percent of the people who subsequently became 'Italians' had no say in the matter. Furthermore, in all probability very few people understood what was happening at the time – a maximum of 10 percent of 'Italians' actually spoke the language, which only become truly national 100 years later. So, not surprisingly, very few people identified with the new Italian state. And a restricted franchise contributed strongly to maintaining a deep hostility between the state and its people – by 1874 the electorate had only risen to 7 percent of the population, and to 8.3 percent in 1909. Universal male suffrage for those over 30 was only granted in 1912. This meant that much working-class opposition was by definition extra-parliamentary.

All of this partly explains the second main factor – the extremely militant, ideologically varied and organisationally chaotic nature of the Italian left.

Very few people had paid much attention to how the 'popular classes' should be treated in a unified country. Among the exceptions was the radical nationalist Giuseppe Mazzini. Although not a socialist, Mazzini was in favour of greater popular participation in politics, and wanted to eradicate poverty and increase literacy. Yet the growing strength of the working class, and particularly the experience of the Paris Commune in 1871, terrified Mazzini and his followers. The long-term consequence of this fear was the beginnings of working-class independence from radical liberals, who themselves slowly moved towards the moderates.

# The growth of anarchism

The main international workers' organisation in this period was the First International, founded by Marx and others in London in 1864. The International grew rapidly in Italy, but on a slightly different basis to many other countries. In 1872 there were 300 branches of the International in Italy, but only two supported Marx's faction. The rest were followers of the Russian anarchist Mikhail Bakunin, who had arrived in Italy in 1864.[1] Such was the strength of Bakunin's following that Frederick Engels complained in 1872 that his stance was 'so simple that it could be learnt by heart in five minutes'.[2]

Simplistic or not, Bakunin's strong following needs to be explained, and the essence of it lies in his determined attempts to gain support among poor peasants – something that the emerging socialist movement systematically failed to do. The First International had originated and developed in the countries of northern Europe, where widespread industrialisation was already under way. But in this period the vast majority of Italian working people still lived in the countryside.

Although the anarchists were more attuned to the needs of the peasants, their crucial error was to massively overestimate peasants' political awareness, often confusing their willingness to rebel in an almost spontaneous fashion with a long-term political project involving the destruction of the state.

In many ways peasant society, and southern Italian society in particular, was at boiling point. So according to the anarchists the local population didn't need to be told they were oppressed and exploited – a spark just had to be thrown into the haystack of their anger. The key tactical move was therefore 'the propaganda of the deed', the launching of secretly prepared insurrections. Two in particular – in 1874 and 1877 – were utter failures, and led to widespread repression and the discrediting of anarchism. These events were turning points in the growth of the Italian left. Although anarchism continued as an important ideological influence for many decades, it was never to return to the degree of strength it had before these failed insurrections.

As Errico Malatesta, who was to remain a leading Italian anarchist activist for 60 years, wrote many years later:

> Because the misery that afflicted the masses was so insufferable, we believed it was enough to give an example, launching with arms in hand the cry of 'Down with the masters', in order for the working masses to fling themselves against the bourgeoisie and take possession of the land, the factories, and all that they produced with their toil and that had been stolen from them.[3]

Another limitation of anarchism was that it was concentrated in the towns and countryside of the South, and had relatively little following in the northern cities, which were then industrialising rapidly. Although industrialisation came late to Italy compared with other European countries, it came swiftly. When Italy was unified in 1860 there were only 2,000 kilometres of railway. But by 1896 the figure had soared to 160,000, driving the expansion of the iron and steel industries. Urbanisation also grew rapidly, with 40 percent of the population living in towns by 1901.

This growing working-class movement in the North came to be dominated by Socialists, led by a young lawyer named Filippo Turati. While in later decades he was to become an inveterate reformist and parliamentarian, Turati's early years were marked by repression and imprisonment. He first came to prominence when he set up a group named *Critica Sociale* in 1891, together with a Russian former anarchist, Anna Kuliscioff.

# The birth of the Socialist Party

This group was one of the key forces behind the birth of the Socialist Party, which was to take on its permanent name in 1895, the *Partito Socialista Italiano* (PSI). Its founding conference, held in Genoa in August 1892, was a great victory for Turati. Three social forces were broadly represented – rank and file peasants who had been influenced by anarchism, the working class of the North influenced by vague notions of socialism, and intellectuals from a middle-class background. But it was a far from unitary affair – there were many anarchist delegates whose behaviour created a very tense atmosphere. Turati managed to create a split during this first conference, so that two separate conferences ended up meeting in the city at two different venues, both of which founded separate political parties. Turati stated at the Socialist conference: 'The programme of a party must be built from its head, not from its feet. You shouldn't fear that a head blocks the movement of the feet – on the contrary, it guides them'.[4]

It was Turati's PSI that was destined to move its head and feet, and to last. In the 1895 election, although voting was still severely restricted, the PSI gained 12 MPs – rising to 35 MPs two years later, with its total vote rising from 26,000 to 135,000.[5] In 1896 it had 20,000 members and a daily newspaper, *Avanti!* (*Forward!*).

All these rapid developments in political organisation were also reflected in workplace organisation. Non-agricultural strikes rose from 27 in 1880 to 139 in 1890, mainly concentrated in textiles and construction.[6] The first *Camera del lavoro*, or trades council, was set up in Milan in 1890, directly inspired by the founding of the Second International the same year. Italian trades councils, much stronger than their British counterparts, organised trade unions at a local level. All these organisational developments among workers, and increasing industrialisation, led to a rapid rise in workers' self-confidence. For example May Day was first celebrated by a city-wide general strike in Milan in 1892, and was organised by a united workers' committee.[7]

Strikes were already numerous before the turn of the century. For instance, a strike wave in 1896 led to a reduction in the working day from ten to nine hours.[8] In May 1898 bread shortages sparked off a virtual insurrection in Milan and, as a result of artillery fire on unarmed crowds, 80 people were killed and 450 wounded, according to official figures.[9] Repression continued after the bloodshed, with Turati being sentenced to 12 years imprisonment, just one of 600 people sentenced by special military tribunals.

In other words, violence and imprisonment were common events for many Socialist leaders of the time – the very individuals who were to play a key role during fascism's rise to power. Indeed, Turati was twice elected as an MP while in jail, and the mayor of Milan elected in 1899 was the father of one of the demonstrators killed in the repression of the previous year. All kinds of rights were frequently trampled upon. For a while the Socialist Party was banned, as well as trades councils.

The trade union movement was mushrooming at the same time. At the first national congress of the metal workers' union (FIOM), held in Livorno in June 1901, calls were made for laws banning child and female labour, the extension of primary education, and pension reform.

In the June 1900 elections the PSI gained 33 seats, winning 13 percent of the vote.[10] By now it had a clearly reformist outlook, most strongly represented by Turati, who was primarily concerned with electioneering and the extension of the franchise. The sum total of all its demands became known as the party's 'Minimum Programme', whose essence was agreed upon at the Rome PSI conference in 1900:

> (1) Political transformation, that is the search for a democratic state where the proletariat really feels politically and juridically equal to the capitalist…
>
> (2) Economic transformation for the social defence of wage earners, aiming at obtaining laws eliminating competition within the working class.
>
> (3) Administrative and financial transformation through all those reforms and institutions which from outside the fields contemplated in the two previous headings raise the value of the proletarian as a man and a citizen, improve his conditions as a consumer, and provide the indispensable financial means for the other reforms already indicated.[11]

But the party was far from being totally dominated by open reformists such as Turati. Many activists understood that it could not grow by only stressing elections, as one delegate at the Rome conference complained: 'Except for the electoral moments when the activity of the branches is truly marvellous, the life of the party is slack and the meetings – even when called to discuss interesting questions close to the poor – are almost deserted'.[12]

In other words, many rank and file members understood that electoralism was far from being sufficient activity. And on a broader, more ideological level, those who came from a Marxist, anarchist or revolutionary syndicalist tradition argued for a revolutionary 'Maximum Programme'. (A similar division was also taking place within the German Social Democratic Party, the SPD.) And indeed, in an attempt to keep the party united, the Rome conference also agreed on its 'Maximum Programme', which talked about conquest of power, expropriation, and the socialisation of the means of production. Supporters of this became known as 'maximalists'.

The official committee report of the Rome conference spoke of the 'Minimum Programme' being the means to the ends outlined in the 'Maximum Programme'. Yet in essence these were two different paths aimed at two different outcomes – parliamentary reforms or revolutionary change. The long-term weakness of such an agreement within the party was that it institutionalised internal division rather than creating unity. What this meant in the future – and this became a crucial factor – was indecisiveness at vital moments.

The PSI had another crucial weakness. It was generally unwilling to work among peasants, although they constituted the vast majority of the working population. Partly this was a result of the historic influence of anarchism, and partly it was a mechanical reading of Marx and the simple hope that industrialisation would remove the need to organise peasants. The PSI forlornly hoped that middle-class members living in or near the countryside would agitate and recruit among peasants – something they were largely incapable of doing. But as a PSI member prophetically stated in 1893: 'It would be madness to await a grandiose development of industrial socialism and only then to make propaganda efforts in the countryside'.[13] Nearly 30 years later, in the *biennio rosso* of 1919-20, and the rise of fascism during 1921-22, the lack of a strong Socialist presence among the peasantry made itself deeply felt.

During this 30-year period the party remained in the hands of the parliamentary reformists. In the years leading up to the First World War many of its senior leaders became incorporated within existing parliamentary and constitutional structures, accepting 'welfare state' type social improvements in the north of the country in exchange for letting the government have a free hand in the South. The price the PSI paid was to support the government in parliamentary votes of confidence – or, put more crudely, PSI votes kept the government alive at crucial moments. Relations sometimes got so close that the prime minister of the time, Giovanni Giolitti, even offered PSI leader Turati a place in his cabinet in 1903, although Turati turned it down.

This moderation was undoubtedly one of the reasons behind the fall in the PSI vote in the 1904 elections, with the party only winning 29 seats. However, by 1909 it gained 20 percent of the vote and 41 seats. Its percentage of votes and representation were even higher in council elections.

The culmination of collaboration with the government occurred in 1911, when the PSI accepted full male suffrage in return for backing the government's invasion of Libya in a vote of confidence. (The background to this was that industrialisation of the country had placed Italy in the role of a minor imperialist power in the Mediterranean and North Africa by the end of the century. Italy had already occupied Abyssinia (Eritrea) as early as 1885, and was anxious not to miss out on the land being grabbed by other European powers.) Echoing what had happened to similar parties, such as the Social Democrats in Germany, Giolitti accurately described the PSI as having 'sent Karl Marx up into the attic'.[14]

The behaviour of the party leadership caused uproar. And the war shocked many people. It was the first time in history that aerial bombardment was used – bombs were dropped against Arabs fighting Italian troops near Tripoli. Thanks to their opposition, the revolutionary left achieved a massive leap forward in terms of their popularity within the party, and among its voters and supporters. One of their emerging leaders was none other than Benito Mussolini, who was even imprisoned for five months for leading some of the protests. The imperialist adventure in Libya was so obvious and distasteful to so many people that at the party congress in July 1912 the revolutionaries achieved a majority.

Mussolini's violent attacks against militarism and bourgeois society in general gained him further support, and allowed him to become editor of the party daily, *Avanti!*. He led moves at the congress to expel right-wing leaders, and witheringly attacked the 'parliamentary cretinism' of many Socialist leaders. Revolutionaries, such as Mussolini, were in the majority within the party until the First World War. A further complication, however, was that the trade union movement remained under the control of reformists, leading to further tensions and squabbles.

But there were already signs of Mussolini's superficial radicalism. Turati wrote of him prophetically in early 1913: 'His voice doesn't emerge from the reality of things, and neither is it inspired by socialism'.[15] Mussolini was a demagogue, often making appeals on the basis of moral outrage. One of the first signs of his move away from socialism was his founding of a fortnightly magazine named *Utopia* in November 1913, aimed at both a 'revolutionary revision' of Marxism and the definition of revolution as 'an act of faith'.[16]

What still remained central for many Socialist leaders were reformist struggles within parliament, not struggles within workplaces and in the streets which would lead to a revolutionary change in society. One author has described Socialist leader Turati's strategy in the following terms: 'He believed that the Socialists could divide the bourgeoisie through parliamentary action in the interests of the working class. This became the reformist credo'.[17]

As was the case with many other socialist parties throughout Europe, including the trade unions and the Labour Party in Britain, a separation was emerging between workplace struggles and parliamentary struggles. Better working conditions were to be achieved by passing progressive laws, and this was the work of parliamentary parties. Trade unions were starting to concentrate on wage rises and defending workers from sackings.

These tendencies were less developed in Italy than elsewhere for two main reasons. Firstly, the level of repression was so high that it was difficult to sustain the notion that parliament and the state could be trusted. As people were shot, leaders arrested and organisations banned, the concept of 'class war' seemed close to home for many workers. While Turati and other supporters had won a significant victory with their 'Minimum Programme', the brutality of the Italian state and industrialisation meant that support for 'maximalism' remained strong.

Secondly, the traditions of Italian workers were often more militant than in many other countries, although sometimes consciousness was a bit raw. One of the major influences within the labour movement and the PSI was anarchism and revolutionary syndicalism. In the early years of the century syndicalism, which spurned 'parliamentary politics' in favour of direct action, came close to becoming the major current within the PSI.

According to syndicalists: 'The proletariat must not settle for gains within the system, jeopardising the chance for radical change… The proletariat could redeem Italy only if it remained autonomous, developing its own values and institutions, as separate as possible from the other classes'.[18] For revolutionary syndicalists, close involvement in struggles for political reforms could constitute a trap in the long term, in which activists would be sucked into accepting the best the current system had to offer. This meant that, on a day to day basis, 'politics' was left to the reformists. Many of these arguments were being played out in other countries, such as between syndicalists and the newly formed British Labour Party:

> Syndicalism had no answer to the generalised political arguments of Labour, because it rejected 'politics' in principle. Its only policy was a spontaneous general strike. Theoretical weakness did not seem to matter when wages were the issue, but as soon as it was a question of going beyond economic action the syndicalists found themselves unarmed, with Labour occupying the high ground of general ideas. *The syndicalists made the fatal mistake of writing off the politics of reformism.*[19]

But, unlike syndicalists in other countries, the Italians were prepared to remain in a political party, even though they felt that industrial struggle was the primary method of achieving revolutionary change. Indeed, Arturo Labriola, the principal theoretician of syndicalism, even stood for parliament in 1904.

# Trade unions and working-class struggle before the First World War

While the fighting instincts of revolutionary syndicalists were exemplary, the impact of their actions was sometimes negative. The best example was Italy's first national general strike, organised by revolutionary syndicalists in September 1904. Some form of mass response became inevitable during this period, as the police were continually killing strikers and demonstrators – and indeed it was the umpteenth police massacre in Sardinia, which saw three striking miners killed, that detonated this strike wave. Crucially, the PSI and trade union leaders delayed calling action, and this allowed revolutionary syndicalists, through their control of many local trades councils, to create the momentum for nationwide action. Strikes broke out city by city, in an uncoordinated and spontaneous fashion, lasting four to five days. Gondoliers stopped work in Venice, workers shut off the power supply in Genoa, barricades were built in Turin and 20,000 marched in Rome, while in Milan public order was virtually in the hands of workers patrolling the streets with trades council armbands.

Indeed, in Milan tens of thousands of workers met every morning in a sports stadium to discuss what form the strike should take. Socialist and trade union leaders argued for a three-day protest strike, while the revolutionary syndicalists called for an indefinite general strike until the government resigned.[20] The reality of the situation was such that, given the militancy of the strike, the more radical proposal was essentially threatening state power. The arguments were thrashed out every morning, but no preparation had been made to systematically take on state forces. Hundreds of thousands of workers had walked out spontaneously, largely unaware of what was happening in other cities. These were not the conditions for launching a revolution. Furthermore a key section of workers, the railwaymen, were not even on strike, and there were no signs of mutinies within the police and armed forces.

Prime minister Giovanni Giolitti simply sat and waited. Rather than inflame the situation he kept the army inside their barracks, and waited until workers began to sense their lack of coordination and leadership. Not surprisingly, a wave of repression and demoralisation followed. Then he called a general election, which he won with an increased majority because progressive middle-class opinion had been frightened by the general strike.

Despite setbacks such as September 1904, radicalism continued to grow within workplaces – conditions were harsh, repression could be savage, and hundreds of thousands of workers were being thrust into the brutality of factory life without feeling any allegiance towards a parliament they had no stake in, or a trade union bureaucracy they had never heard of.

All these factors conditioned both trade union and Socialist leaders. The Italian equivalent of the TUC, the CGL, was founded in 1906, partly to ward off the influence of syndicalism. This helped to reinforce a more conservative leadership within both the trade union bureaucracy and the PSI. According to the classic formulation, 'economic' struggles were to be led by the CGL, 'political' struggles by the PSI. By 1911 membership of the CGL had reached 384,000.[21] However, the overall situation was that the vast majority of workers were not even in trade unions. The best organised group, metal workers in the FIOM union, only had 21 percent of the workforce as members of their union.[22] Nevertheless, the influence of syndicalism remained strong. The following year syndicalists created their own trade union federation, the USI, with 80,000 to 100,000 members including the national rail workers' union with 25,000 members, and the 18,000 members of the Parma trades council. At its second congress in December 1913 the USI claimed more than 100,000 members.[23]

Most of the world economy was in recession in the years leading up to the First World War, so employers frequently reneged on many of the agreements they had signed with workers. This led to widespread strikes before the war, culminating in the 'Red Week' of June 1914. The spark came when a demonstration in the eastern port of Ancona, organised by Socialists and anarchists, was fired on by the police and three people were killed. The country exploded:

> The PSI, in accordance with its policy, called a general strike. This was the signal for insurrectionary outbreaks. Ancona was held by rebels for 10 days. Barricades went up in all the big cities. In Emilia and the Marches, authority collapsed. Local leaders established the dictatorship of the proletariat – red flags were raised, churches attacked, railways torn up, villas sacked, taxes abolished and prices reduced. The socialist state within a state in Emilia became reality, and it took 10,000 troops to reduce Ancona. The extent and the intensity of the strike were without precedent. There was no effective central leadership – socialists, anarchists, syndicalists and republicans joined in a melée.[24]

A pattern, which would become familiar, was now established – the PSI leadership would do nothing to take the movement forward. And although this movement was defeated, the speed and scale of its dynamic showed everyone that industrialisation had created a new militant working class, which was to take centre stage in 1919-20. The problem for the ruling class was to find some means of taming this new and sometimes leaderless movement.

# The First World War and the crisis of Italian democracy

When the First World War broke out in September 1914 Italy was in alliance with Germany and Austria-Hungary, but remained neutral until May 1915. Yet when Italy entered the war it did so on the opposite side, joining the Anglo-French-Russian alliance.

Such a turnaround needs some explaining. First of all, Italy's economic growth over the previous 20 years had fuelled a desire to expand into the Balkans, a move resisted by Austria-Hungary. Furthermore, German capital had penetrated Italy significantly; many major Italian banks had come under the control of German financiers in this period. Yet another international reason for the ruling class to join the 'other side' was that Britain, through its control of Gibraltar and Suez, now controlled the export and import of raw materials through the Mediterranean.

But the decision to join the war was also caused by domestic reasons. Some elements in the ruling class hoped that the inevitable tide of nationalism that war brings would help to undermine support for the Socialist Party. Equally as important, and linked to this, was the political desire to get rid of Giovanni Giolitti and his 'system', which included the incorporation of the PSI within the parliamentary system, and potentially the idea that PSI members might one day end up in government. As early as 1904 the nationalist Vilfredo Pareto had understood the potential usefulness of war: 'If there is a big European war socialism will be off the agenda for at least 50 years, and at the same time the bourgeoisie will be safe'.[25] Ultra-nationalists, understanding that they were now living in 'the age of the masses', hoped that nationalist drum-beating over war would enable working-class people to be captured 'from the right' rather than from the left.

Other calls for intervention in the war were made by the nationalist poet Gabriele D'Annunzio and the very influential Futurist movement, which was generally under the sway of nationalist and right-wing ideas.

There were also those who claimed involvement in the war could be a 'preliminary revolution', such as Benito Mussolini, by now a major PSI leader, editor of its daily *Avanti!*, and councillor in Milan. In other words the experience of war and its destabilising effects would inevitably sweep away the staid political regime led by Giolitti, providing massive political opportunities for those who were prepared to take them. Furthermore, at this time Mussolini and many others feared an Austro-Hungarian invasion and viewed its decaying empire as a particularly reactionary state, and were caught up in romantic visions of revolutionary France, cradle of revolution. Just as he was the most extreme oppositionist to the Libyan war, Mussolini now became the most extreme supporter of Italian participation in the First World War.

Mussolini found common ground with a surprisingly large

number of revolutionary syndicalists, who claimed that the Italian working class had an 'international duty' to take part in the war against German and Austro-Hungarian reaction through joining an alliance with France, Britain and (the very reactionary) Russia. Underlying all this was a more important political development among the syndicalists – the end of their belief in the revolutionary potential of the working class. It wouldn't be mass workers' action that would lead to a revolutionary change in society, but an imperialist war. Such sudden shifts were not new: even when leading workers' struggles, syndicalists had often been adventurist. Yet on this occasion very few heeded their call – most industrial and agricultural workers remained anti-war or neutral.

In any event, Mussolini first came out in favour of intervention in an article he wrote in *Avanti!* on 18 October 1914, entitled 'From Absolute Neutrality to Active and Operational Neutrality', in which he began to argue that one side in the war could be considered more progressive than the other. As ever, he strongly attacked the passivity and immobility of the PSI leadership. He was forced to resign as editor three days later and, although he had been very popular, was expelled from the party following pressure from the rank and file. A meeting of PSI activists in Milan had reduced Mussolini to tears, with hundreds spitting on him and calling him a traitor.

His next move saw the beginning of a relationship that was to prove crucial a few years later: industrialists agreed to finance his request to set up a right-wing daily newspaper, *Il Popolo d'Italia* (*The People of Italy*), which first appeared in November 1914. He also received finance from France, a potential military ally if Italy were to go to war. Mussolini's new paper frequently used quotes from French historical figures such as Blanqui and Napoleon, such as 'He who has steel has bread!' or 'Revolution is an idea which has found bayonets!' On 31 March 1915 he led a pro-war march in Milan that was opposed by the PSI – indeed, PSI leader Serrati and another 200 Socialists were arrested during their counter-demonstration.

Following the ideas of the French syndicalist Georges Sorel,

Mussolini was also moving to the conclusion that democracy itself was a problem – the conventions of parliament held back revolutionary change. A few years later, just four days before taking power in October 1922 as the leader of fascism, Mussolini stated that fascism was 'supreme anti-democracy'.[26]

The problem for all these forces was that there was mass opposition to the war. Despite its many weaknesses, the PSI had remained quite internationalist in character. At the outbreak of the First World War it did not follow the same line as the rest of Europe's socialist and social-democratic parties, in voting support for 'their' governments, but instead called for 'neither support nor sabotage'. The only two left parties to completely oppose the war were the Serbian social democrats and the Bolshevik Party in Russia. Indeed, Lenin defined the PSI as the 'happy exception'. Furthermore, the country's leading politician, Giovanni Giolitti, was also against the war.

So the eight months between the start of general hostilities in Europe and Italy's declaration of war were months of intense political debate. And the months immediately preceding the war, particularly the 'Red Week' of June 1914, were also a period of immense social upheaval. There could be nothing like a good old-fashioned war to stop strikes and bring 'the nation' together.

But such was the shambolic practice of the PSI, and its chaotic political line, that many activists were swayed into believing that a war could have some positive aspects. The future leader of the Italian Communist Party (PCI) Palmiro Togliatti left the PSI upon the outbreak of war and joined up, although he was sent to the medical corps on health grounds. In October 1914 a young activist named Antonio Gramsci wrote an ambiguous article which many people labelled as 'interventionist', and which was to haunt him for many years.[27] This is not to say that all Social-ists were pro-war, far from it – in Naples the group around Amadeo Bordiga never wavered in its anti-war position for a moment.

Even up to a week before the declaration of war, the majority of MPs, in agreement with Giolitti, were officially against the war. What is important was how this situation was turned round: 'Giolitti's mistake was that of believing that the decisive issues would be resolved in the parliamentary arena, and therefore within an environment in which he had a loyal majority'.[28] Two factors came into play in order to turn the tables – parliamentary and institutional manoeuvres, and mass demonstrations. These same two factors again came into play seven years later when the establishment invited Mussolini to become prime minister.

When parliament voted for war credits the PSI voted against. But in a typical manoeuvre, Turati then privately offered senior politicians 'dignified collaboration' and promised to keep the working class in line with the 'national interest'.

In any event, war turned the country upside down. Some 5.9 million Italians were conscripted, with 4 million alone being sent to the Italian-Austrian border. Southern peasants conscripted as soldiers were promised land after the war, but in the trenches many came across northern Socialists for the first time, and began to be influenced by arguments against the war. Even Mussolini, who had joined up, confessed in his diary that most soldiers had never even heard of concepts such as 'neutrality' and 'intervention' in the war, writing: 'They accept [the war] as a duty and don't talk about it. I've never heard people speaking about neutrality or intervention. I believe that many soldiers, as they come from remote villages, have not even heard of these words'.[29]

Conditions in the trenches were terrible. Towards the end of the war thousands of peasants wrote postcards back home, urging their fellow villagers to burn or destroy the crops, thus causing an economic crisis that would bring the war to an end.

Army commanders were almost as much at war against their own troops as they were against the 'enemy'. Military tribunals passed 210,000 sentences during the war, 10,000 alone for the offence of self-mutilation. Desertions increased, and in some cases the military authorities began a policy of decimation – killing one soldier in 10 in order to raise morale! It has been estimated that up to 2,000 soldiers were shot as part of the policy of decimation. One of the worst cases was the execution of 30 soldiers from the Ravenna Brigade in March 1917.

Fighting in this area of Europe was every bit as monotonous, bloody and pointless as on the Western Front. For example in May and June 1917 the tenth major battle was fought out in the Isonzo area, in the extreme north east of Italy. Two months later, in October, Italy suffered a disastrous defeat at Caporetto, when 33 army divisions retreated in disarray. The generals had ignored warnings that Austrian forces had been reinforced with German troops in preparation for a rapid breakout, and were also caught totally by surprise by the use of mustard gas.

The military command unleashed a wave of executions on the soldiers retreating in disorder from the battle – up to 5,000 were shot without trial.[30] In just a few weeks 10,000 Italian troops were killed, 300,000 wounded and 300,000 captured, as the Austrians drove 70 miles into Italian territory.[31] Another 350,000 deserted and returned home – Italy had lost half its army.[32]

In order to cover up their incompetence, the generals and the government started to invent myths about the 'enemy within', ie the Socialists, who still had an official policy towards the war of 'neither support nor sabotage'. Attempts were made to ban the party's daily paper, but when that failed the editor, Serrati, was given a jail sentence for the crime of 'pacifist propaganda'.

All of this led to the left flipping over and supporting the war effort. The CGL's official journal stated: 'When the enemy treads on our soil we have only one duty – to resist.' And at the height of the Caporetto crisis Turati declared that the territory around the front line was as sacred to Socialists as to any other Italian.[33]

# The creation of the *Arditi*

In the summer of 1917 General Capello and Lieutenant-Colonel Bassi of the Second Army created special assault brigades to break through enemy lines. On 12 June in Russig, behind the Gorizia front, a specially armed and trained company of volunteers was formed.[34] These volunteers were given slightly better accommodation, higher wages, exemption from normal trench duty and longer periods of leave, and were allowed to receive visitors and gifts.[35] These troops, known as *Arditi*, quickly became a very separate body from the rest of the army.

These privileges were given because the risks were greater – the

*Arditi* were primarily assault troops who attacked enemy lines first. However, enrolment was appealing due to the monotonous and miserable conditions in the trenches. On the eve of the major defeat at the battle of Caporetto, the Second Army already had 6,000 *Arditi*. Other armies had another 20 assault brigades.[36] However, other battles saw very high losses: only 180 out of 400 *Arditi* came back from the battle of San Michele.[37]

Political ideas were quite openly voiced in these formations. While it is true to say that many *Arditi* did become fascists, fascism did not exist in the trenches – it was born after the end of the war. However, the nationalist Futurist movement, which already existed, influenced many *Arditi*. Another common attitude, a mixture of rebelliousness and elitism, was hatred of the military police (*carabinieri*), many of whom were killed by *Arditi*.[38] What began worrying military and political leaders was the attempt by left-wing organisations to politicise the *Arditi*. General Diaz wrote of his concerns to prime minister Vittorio Emanuele Orlando on 18 May 1918: 'I can see how the creation of links between *Arditi* and subversive parties can be worrying in view of the return to the civilian life of these men. Therefore I will continue to carefully monitor all examples of attempted recruitment of our troops by extremist committees'.[39] Two months before, the nationalist officer Luigi Federzoni wrote in more worrying tones to the prime minister: 'Among the soldiers, and especially the *Arditi*, the tendency has developed of carrying out reprisals and vendettas against the *carabinieri*, who are quietly identified as being policemen, but above all *cowards who avoid the front line*'.[40]

It was attitudes such as these that led to many soldiers having to wait a year before being allowed to return to civilian life. Some were sent to put down a revolt in Albania, others were ordered on repeated forced marches, and many caught malaria or the deadly 'Spanish' flu of the time. This treatment only increased their alienation from the standard military traditions of discipline and obedience to authority.

The Italian state had hoped it could use the war as a means of regaining social control. Giolitti had resigned as prime minister in March 1914 because he saw that he was unable to rule effectively.

Although military discipline within factories helped ensure industrial peace, the shortages caused by the war led to unrest in the streets: in 1917 women led a series of bread riots in Turin. Many working-class families had no alternative – the level of real wages fell by 27 percent in 1917 alone. Furthermore, strikes did not really decrease during the war – 673,000 strike days were 'lost' in 1915, the year Italy entered the war, rising to 906,000 in 1918.[41]

Italy had scored no significant military victories in three and a half years of war. Yet 571,000 had been killed, 451,000 were permanently disabled, and another 117,000 died during imprisonment. Although Italy was on the 'winning' side in the war it obtained very few spoils, which only increased dissatisfaction, particularly among the officer class.

When rapid demobilisation occurred from March to November 1919 it coincided with rapidly rising unemployment. For example, in the area around Ferrara – one of the first to witness widespread fascist violence – the local prefect reported as early as February 1919 that crime was rising rapidly, caused mainly by unemployed ex-soldiers.[42]

Factories, meanwhile, were soon to be freed from the military discipline they had endured during the war. The effects of these contradictions were to culminate in what is known as the *biennio rosso*, the 'two red years' of 1919-20.

# The Italian left

## The *biennio rosso*

By the end of the war Italy was at boiling point. The country had not only suffered shortages and privations, it had also experienced rapid and massive industrialisation. During the war the number of people working in Genoa for the steel firm Ansaldo increased from 6,000 to 100,000, while the value of the motor company Fiat rose from 30 million to 500 million lire. Out of a total population of 500,000 in Turin, 200,000 were factory workers.

Heavy industry had made huge profits during the war. Profit rates in the steel industry rose from 6.3 percent in 1915 to 16.7 percent in 1917, in car manufacture from 8.2 percent to 30.5 percent, and in chemicals from 8 percent to over 15 percent.[1] Despite this, at the end of the war industries began to sack workers. As a result many troops returned home to unemployment.

Workers resented the harsh regime they had been subjected to during the war – those who broke factory regulations had sometimes been sent to the front – and many workers were inspired by the Russian Revolution and came under the influence of Socialists.

The PSI had grown from a membership of 50,000 in 1914 to 216,000 in 1921, and from 50 MPs before the war to 156 in 1919, when it became the largest party in parliament. The party's daily, *Avanti!*, sold 300,000 copies a day – 50,000 alone in Turin.[2] Similarly, the largest union federation, the CGL, rose from just below 250,000 members at the end of 1918 to 1 million in 1919 and 2.2 million in 1920.[3] The semi-anarchist, semi revolutionary syndicalist USI federation claimed 500,000 members in 1919, with its main stronghold being the rural areas of the Po valley. It therefore played a relatively minor role in the big industrial disputes.[4] Most of these new recruits to trade unions were radical and prepared to take action, but politically they were inexperienced. They would need guidance at specific moments, and needed to clarify what they understood by socialism and how it would be created. Crucially, as we shall see, the PSI was unable to play a role of true leadership, by explaining complicated circumstances clearly and calling for decisive action at vital turning points.

Despite these limitations, the middle classes were fearful of the general growth in socialism and dismayed that their savings were being wiped out by high inflation. The lira's massive devaluation hit savers hard – in 1920 it was only worth a quarter of its 1914 value. Many people with savings had bought war bonds between 1916 and 1918 for patriotic reasons, yet they found by the end of 1920 that their value had declined by 75 percent.[5] Whatever side of the political spectrum you came from, it was clear that Italy was heading towards profound social strife. Both industrialists and sections of the middle class began looking around for an alternative that would extinguish this wave of rebelliousness.

On the other hand, for the working class the PSI represented a clear alternative to harsh workplace discipline, unemployment and wage cuts. The government was clearly incapable of containing socialism and the growing militancy of workers. After its national success in 1919, in local elections held in September 1920 the PSI gained control of 2,162 of Italy's 8,000 local councils, and 26 out of 69 provincial councils.

It should also be remembered that there had been a successful working-class revolution in Russia two years before, and that soviet republics had been proclaimed in Budapest in March 1919 and in Munich the following month. In other words, revolution was in the air throughout Europe in 1919.

The PSI, though, was a very strange beast. At its congress in October 1919, held just a few weeks before its electoral victory, the 'maximalists' regained control and changed the party's programme to call for 'the conquest of power and for the consolidation of revolutionary conquests'. This would be achieved by a 'transitory regime of the dictatorship of the entire proletariat'.[6] The party continued to pass paper motions about revolution, such as at a PSI national council in April 1920: 'We need to take power today. In order to save itself, the proletariat has to take control. The working class has to seize power by any means necessary, even by spilling blood if needs be'.[7]

These were fine words, but what was being done to turn them into reality? One author has argued:

> Throughout this period, however, nothing was done by the Socialist Party actually to make any preparations for revolution. It made no attempt to clarify, in its own conception, what it meant by slogans borrowed from the Russians... At no time was there anything done...to prepare for seizure of power either through organisation or through planning... With the conditions of Italy at the time, and in the atmosphere of hysterical exhortations it created, the Socialists could not stand still. When they did, they found their influence waning.[8]

The same tendency was reflected within trade unions. At the November 1918 congress of the FIOM engineering union it was stated: 'We have to aim for the greatest democratisation possible within factories, transforming our old Internal Commissions [shop stewards committees] into permanent organs of control, with the power to intervene over all questions regarding work, pay and discipline'.[9] While not a call for revolution, this was undoubtedly a reflection of a growing sense of confidence among the rank and file.

One of the main concrete advances for engineering workers was the gaining of the eight-hour day (over six working days, ie a total of 48 hours) in March 1919, which generally involved a reduction from a 60-hour or 72-hour week. There had been strong support for this, given the very long hours worked in industry during wartime. However, once trade union activists had compelled employers to implement the changes, they then had to fight factory by factory to stop people being forced to work harder. In other words, bosses gave shorter working hours with one hand, and with the other tried to maintain their profit margins by speeding up the production line. Overtime rates had also been raised as part of this agreement, although many workers wanted a total end to overtime on principle.[10]

One writer, describing the profound class tensions that existed in 1919, said: 'The Socialist success in March, together with the conquest of the eight-hour day, did not end but intensified agitations and disputes. It was the overall order of Italian society which was being questioned'.[11]

Although confrontation during the *biennio rosso* was centred upon engineering factories, particularly in Turin, profound class conflict was sweeping the whole nation. In June and July 1919 nationwide protests over food prices reached insurrectionary proportions in some areas. Pietro Nenni, a major PSI leader at the time, later wrote:

> Spontaneous food soviets arose all over Italy. In Emilia, Romagna, Tuscany and the Marches, you could define them as real insur-rections, often with cases of fraternisation between demonstrators and troops. In Florence the masses had control over the city. The general strike (4 July) saw the same thing in Ancona, Bologna, Palermo, etc. Lootings and occupations were taking place from one end of the country to another. Power was transferred to the trades council, to which the owners handed in the keys of their warehouses. But nobody put themselves at the head of the masses, no one sought to give a political voice to the discontent. While the blood flowed, while the soldiers sent to repress them fraternised with the mob, the party leadership limited itself to a stereotyped communication attesting its sympathy to the demonstrators.[12]

In other words, many strikes, demonstrations and revolts broke out independently of Socialist Party leadership. Individual So-cialists were often involved, but the action was not the result of systematic party work. Similarly, the conduct of the dispute did not involve concrete agitation from the Socialist Party at a national level.

It was a period when people were 'strike happy'. In Bologna chaplains even threatened to strike, tired of taking masses at pre-war rates.[13] A far more substantial event was a two-day general strike on 20-21 July, in protest against Allied military intervention against Soviet Russia. Such was the popularity of Russia that in March the traditionally moderate Builders' Federation had voted to join the Third International, only to be told that political parties alone could be members. And such was the level of militancy that many left-wing activists and leaders thought that this strike might be a pretext to a revolution.[14] The fact that leaders could think this, without ever having seen or heard of any detailed plans for an insurrection, was another example of the climate of verbal radicalism and practical confusion.

All of this worried the ruling class intensely. The advent of democracy had led to the Socialist Party becoming the largest party, and workplaces were to a certain extent becoming ungovernable. So even before fascism became a major force, the main employers' association outlined its solution in March 1920:

> The current grave economic situation can only be overcome by an intensification of production, together with a reduction in unnecessary consumption, and for this goal to be reached the government must have a clear, precise and firm strategy which ensures discipline throughout the country and security in terms of the development of free independent initiatives, as well as maintaining the rule of law.[15]

The problem for the authorities was that massive repression had failed to stem the tide. From April 1919 to April 1920, 145 workers had been killed by the forces of 'law and order' and another 444 wounded. One Socialist Party leader noted in December 1919: 'Even before the revolution has taken place, we can feel the chill wind of counter-revolution blowing around us'.[16]

But attacks did not only come in the shape of naked violence. A series of attacks by the authorities and employers began in Spring 1920, with troops being used to drive protesting workers out of Turin factories. Strikes were called in response, shutting down the whole city. Nevertheless, PSI leaders refused to call for solidarity action elsewhere.

The March 'sciopero delle lancette' strike was initially called against the sacking of three workers involved in a dispute about a new timetable, although the real issue quickly became recognition of the factory councils. These new organisations were broader than trade union branches, as people could vote and be elected to them regardless of whether they were in a trade union or not. Furthermore, they demanded the right to intervene in areas outside of the legal contract signed between employer and employees.

The employers sensed that such a broad form of workers' organisation broke through the narrower horizons of traditional trade unionism, and therefore bitterly resisted their creation. The employers' association in Turin invited its members 'to not recognise workers' representative bodies which differ from the normal form of trade unions'.[17] The dispute broadened out to a general strike in the Piedmont region, of which Turin is the capital, lasting 10 days. Solidarity was also seen elsewhere – in Florence, Livorno and Pisa railway workers refused to move troops, and in Genoa and Livorno workers and sailors sabotaged the ports.[18]

Although this strike failed, it put the idea of factory councils on the national political map. Moreover, the militancy of workers and their support for factory councils was undimmed, which explains why the CGL union federation called in its May Day manifesto for 'the creation of bodies appropriate to the running of companies and control over production. We have to insist that factory councils be recognised everywhere, with roles far greater than those which have hitherto been given to shop stewards' committees'.[19]

In the countryside peasants seized land from big landowners, while soldiers mutinied rather than go and fight a new war in Albania. The town of Ancona saw widespread disorder in June 1920, when a regiment refused to be sent to Albania. Fresh troops equipped with tanks, and *carabinieri* with hand grenades, were immediately sent to the town, and in bitter fighting 22 soldiers were killed.[20] Disturbances spread to other towns and regiments, notably further down the east coast at Brindisi, where three days later some *Arditi* who had previously volunteered for service in Albania tried to prevent the departure of their ship, leading to more battles with the police.[21] At the Second Congress of the Third International in Moscow, held in August 1920, PSI leader Serrati claimed that his party was 'so powerful that it may be said that the Italian proletariat is almost ready to seize power'.[22] The huge scale of strike action seems to bear Serrati out:

|                                          | 1919       | 1920          |
|------------------------------------------|-----------:|--------------:|
| Strikes in industry                      | 1,663      | 1,881         |
| Strike days                              | 18,888,000 | 16,398,000    |
| Industrial workers taking strike action  | 1,049,000  | 1,268,000     |
| Strikes in agriculture                   | 208        | 189           |
| Strike days                              | 3,437,000  | 14,171,000    |
| Agricultural workers taking strike action | 505,000   | 1,046,000[23] |

Pay rates increased as a result of all this activity. In 1918 real wages had fallen to 65 percent of their 1913 level, but they rose to 114 percent in 1920 and 127 percent in 1921 – all of this despite a fivefold increase in prices.[24] Striking produced results – in January 1920 post office workers won all their demands, while in the same month railway workers won pay increases and the right to strike.[25]

The culmination of this entire period took place in September 1920, with the occupation of hundreds of engineering plants. The outcome of this occupation was the single most important event in the rise of fascism.

# The occupation of the factories

In June 1920 FIOM, the engineering union, presented a whole series of demands concerning wage increases and changes in salary structures, only to see them all rejected by the employers. A union leader who had negotiated with the bosses later recounted that they were told: 'All discussions are pointless. The industrialists are against granting any pay increase. Since the end of the war we've continually bent over backwards. The time to call a stop has now come'.[26] FIOM responded by ordering an overtime ban, followed in August by a work to rule and a go-slow. If the employers attempted to lock out their workers, the union advised its members to occupy the factories. The anarchist USI federation argued for offensive rather than defensive occupations, and for involving other categories of workers. Although the union had insisted that all actions be kept within the law, open sabotage of production started to take place by mid-August, with production sometimes dropping by 40 percent.

Yet it must be said that the occupations were triggered by the industrialists, who were confident of victory. On 30 August workers were locked out of the Alfa Romeo factory in Milan, and FIOM ordered its members to occupy 300 engineering factories across the city. The anarchist leader Errico Malatesta commented: 'If we let this favourable moment pass, we shall later pay with tears of blood for the fear we have instilled in the bourgeoisie'.[27]

Once again, the Socialist Party found itself reacting to events rather than agitating for them. But, as the main Milan newspaper reported, the first day of what became a wave of occupations must have immediately dented the employers' confidence:

> The factories yesterday evening presented a singular spectacle. One reached them through crowds of women and children, coming and going with dinner for the strikers… Entrances were strictly guarded by groups of workers. Not the ghost of an official or police officer in sight. The strikers were complete masters of the field. Whoever passed, in a car or cab, was subjected to control as if he were crossing a frontier, with control exercised by vigilance squads of workers and their enthusiastic companions.[28]

But despite what the journalist might have thought, women were not just bringing in food. A shop steward and member of the Turin trades council recalled many years later:

> We used to go to the Fiat *Grandi Motori* factory to get guns and ammunition, and then take them to the Red Guards in our factory… If we didn't do this they might have attacked us. By 1920 there were already a few fascist squads around. You hardly ever saw them, but they were there… We had made some long shopping bags, like our grandmothers had, and we put the ammunition inside them and then under our clothes.[29]

In Milan alone 280 factories were now occupied. As workers pored over management records, they uncovered evidence of systematic blacklisting of union and political activists, thus making the action far more than just a wages dispute.[30]

Many occupations attempted to continue production under workers' control. In Turin there was a fixed meeting place where occupation committees could discuss supplying raw materials and components to each other's factories.[31] Railway workers often ensured they were supplied with fuel, iron and steel – indeed, the Turin manager of state railways complained by phone to the national railway boss in Rome: 'In effect, what's taking shape here, and there are various signs of it, is a takeover of the railways… They say they are the bosses these days'.[32] In Turin the main Fiat factory was producing 37 cars a day, half the normal level of production,[33] while others were producing more than in an earlier period of go-slows. Not only were workers demanding that production be restarted under workers' control, they also wanted goods to be sold to Soviet Russia.

However, there were no plans for an insurrection, or even offensive actions such as seizing other weapons or storming public buildings. Nevertheless, in the space of just a few days, at least in the major industrial cities, the notion that working-class people could run their own affairs became a reality.

The boss of Fiat, Giovanni Agnelli, had anguished conversations about his factories with prime minister Giolitti, who was prepared to bombard the factories. As the following conversation makes clear, while it was impractical to storm armed workers barricaded inside factories, any bombardment would cause severe economic losses to Agnelli:

Giolitti: To drive the workers out of the factories, we need artillery…
Agnelli: I agree…
G: We are in a position to supply it immediately. At Turin, there is the seventh regiment of mountain artillery. I will give the orders at once. At dawn tomorrow, Fiat will be bombarded and liberated from the occupiers.
A: No! No!…

G: Well, then?
A: (No reply.)[34]

The strike therefore quickly came to threaten state power. The prefect of Turin, the epicentre of the struggle, cabled Rome explaining that 'there are 800 officers and 35 mounted officers facing 72,000 engineering workers', and asked for advice. His problem was that these 72,000 workers were barricaded inside their factories, so the traditional solution of cavalry charges was not an option.

With traditional means of repression ruled out, and no immediate electoral contest to distract attention, the sense of foreboding increased among industrialists and establishment politicians. On 5 September the CGL union federation, in agreement with the PSI, issued a statement in which it demanded that employers immediately concede pay rises, otherwise action would be escalated and would involve 'control over workplaces in order to obtain collective management and the socialisation of all forms of production'.

Half a million engineering workers were now occupying their factories. Then chemical and shoe factories were occupied in Milan, while in Turin chemical and textile factories were also occupied.[35] At the very same time the largest party in the country, the PSI, was continually talking about revolution. On 7 September the PSI daily headlined with the message: 'Perhaps the decisive moment is imminent. Workers of Italy, discipline, organise and arm yourselves!'[36]

On the other hand, the bosses were still refusing to make any concessions.

Yet instead of leading the movement forward in the direction they had promised, trade union and PSI leaders suddenly engaged in a cynical 'pass the parcel' series of meetings and congresses that culminated on 10 September, when two motions were presented to a meeting of the CGL leadership. The PSI motion called for the movement to be put under its control, so that it would move 'towards the maximum solution of the socialist programme'. Another even vaguer motion was presented by CGL leaders which talked about 'union control' over production. The union leaders' motion won by 591,245 to 409,569 votes. Predictably, PSI leaders then cynically accused the unions of 'betraying' the revolution.

Apart from being the home of Fiat and engineering militancy, Turin was also the base of a growing revolutionary grouping within the PSI. Its initial instigator was Angelo Tasca, who gathered other young activists around him such as Antonio Gramsci, Palmiro Togliatti and Umberto Terracini. These young revolutionaries launched a new weekly socialist newspaper, *Ordine Nuovo* (*New Order*) on May Day 1919, with Gramsci as editor, which by August was already selling just over 3,000. It was read mainly in Turin, and was largely distributed by direct selling, often in PSI branches.[37]

The *Ordine Nuovo* group had another advantage which came about due to a local peculiarity of the still sizeable anarchist movement. On a national level anarchist trade unionists were active within their own USI federation, but as this had never been built in Turin, anarchists were simply part of the normal union structure. For example, a prominent anarchist, Pietro Ferrero, was secretary of the Turin branch of FIOM, the engineering union. While Ferrero had many theoretical disagreements with Gramsci over communism,[38] he, like many other anarchists in Turin, was often fully convinced of the importance of factory councils, and equally mistrustful of Socialist and trade union bureaucrats.[39]

Although the distribution of *Ordine Nuovo* was relatively small, its influence ran far wider. But nevertheless, the *Ordine Nuovo* group did not want to risk launching an insurrection which would have questionable support at a national level. As Palmiro Togliatti, one of Gramsci's group, argued at the 10 September CGL meeting:

> You must not count on an action developed from Turin alone. We will not attack alone. To be able to attack, a simultaneous action from the countryside and above all a national action would be necessary. We want to be assured on this point because otherwise we do not want to commit our proletariat.[40]

With hindsight it is clear that Gramsci and his *Ordine Nuovo* group were isolated; they did not have a national structure. Furthermore they were inexperienced – for example, at the start of 1919 Palmiro Togliatti was essentially unknown within the Turin Socialist Party – although by August he was secretary of the PSI Federation in Turin. The *Ordine Nuovo* group was also very young. In 1920 Gramsci, aged 28, was the oldest of the leading group. Tasca was 27, Terracini 24 and Togliatti 26.

The occupation ended in compromise. Socialist leader Serrati commented at the time: 'For now the bosses are giving in – they are going to pay for wage increases, annual holidays and back pay'.[41] The anarchist leader Armando Borghi stressed the disorientation of many workers: 'Afterwards many trade unionists felt they had been defeated, but in a confused way. They didn't understand clearly either how or by whom – so they continued to believe that they hadn't been defeated'.[42]

Mussolini, however, took a longer-term perspective, commenting that the PSI did not know how 'to profit from a revolutionary situation such as history does not repeat'.[43] And over the coming two years it would be Mussolini who profited enormously from the wasted opportunity of the occupation.

# The Socialist/Communist split

The mutual recriminations within the PSI over the failure to make greater capital out of the occupation of the factories were intense. For example, the PSI leadership quickly closed down the Turin news desk of *Avanti!*, where Gramsci and other *Ordine Nuovo* supporters worked.

For radicals such as Gramsci a revolutionary chance had been wasted because Socialist Party leaders did not want to lead it. And it must be said that most PSI leaders had a rather mechanical view of socialism – ie socialism was inevitable, the crisis of capitalism was inevitable, there would come a time when conditions were ripe for socialism, and so on. The PSI had grown on the basis of vague rhetoric about revolution, and when a concrete opportunity presented itself in September 1920 it did not further the movement. Trotsky commented: 'The PSI verbally conducted a revolutionary policy, without ever taking into account any of its consequences. Everybody knows that during the September events no other organisation so lost its head and became so paralysed by fear as the PSI which had itself paved the way for these events'.[44]

Socialists outside of Turin and other industrial cities, such as in the agricultural town of Ferrara, understood that the constant vacillations of Turati and other Socialist leaders were becoming impossible to support. Writing in a local Socialist paper in mid-August, the editor expressed the frustration of many party members:

> Even though we are not a step nearer to the revolution, even though a condition of unease is obvious because of the contradiction between our words and our actions, even though the people begin to be disoriented and disappointed…even though the bourgeoisie is regaining its internal strength and organising its white guard against the proletariat which has no red guard, Turati can't offer us anything better than the old method. Ah, no! For god's sake![45]

The failure of the occupation of the factories made it clear to many Socialists that not only was a revolution quite a distance away, it was also a very complex and arduous process. For other leaders such as Amadeo Bordiga, the failures, ambiguities and empty rhetoric of PSI leaders clearly demonstrated the need to form a 'purer' party, a communist party. A communist faction within the PSI was subsequently announced at a meeting in Imola on 29 November 1920 – a faction that was to be dominated by Bordiga and his followers.

So the left may have been divided, but it was still powerful and confident. The occupation of the factories had showed both that it was capable of threatening the very basis of how society was governed, and that the ruling class had no immediate hope of stopping it by conventional means. Nevertheless, the establishment and the middle classes were determined to destroy this power by any means necessary.

# The rise of fascism

While the left debated the failure of the occupation of the factories, industrialists and large landowners moved into action. They had looked into the abyss of working-class revolution and were terrified. Given the inability of conventional parliamentary politics to protect their class interests, they began to look to more extreme options. The existing government could not contain inflation, economic collapse or the Socialist Party. And, to add to their problems, the Communist Party was born in January 1921.

Mussolini and his fascist movement, founded at a meeting of 118 people held in Milan on 23 March 1919, vowed to bring an end to 'lawlessness'. Mussolini was promising strong government and the regaining of Italy's national pride. Yet at the founding meeting of the movement the programme agreed upon also called for universal suffrage with a proportional voting system, votes for women, the abolition of the Senate, an eight-hour day, a minimum wage and retirement at 55.[1] A further programme issued in June also called for the confiscation of all church property, a progressive tax on capital, an 85 percent tax on war profits, the nationalisation of munitions factories, and workers' participation in joint management schemes.[2]

Not surprisingly, some of the early fascists came from the working class. But many were ex-soldiers, particularly officers. They resented the organised working class which had sat the war out in factories, and which was now striking for higher wages and better conditions at work, while many ex-soldiers were unemployed. They were also angry about the industrialists who had made huge profits during the war. Mussolini was quick to sense their discontent and, as part of a deeper shift, on 1 August 1918 he changed the subtitle of his daily *Il Popolo d'Italia* from 'Socialist newspaper' to 'Newspaper of veterans and producers'.

The military high command even facilitated the distribution of the newspaper among the army.[3]

Perhaps the first backer of Mussolini's fascist movement was the British government. In 1917 Samuel Hoare, who was to become foreign secretary in the 1930s, was a military intelligence officer in northern Italy. Once he understood what Mussolini was about, he asked the director of Military Intelligence in the London Foreign Office to support the movement:

> He agreed, and gave me the means of subsidising a resistance movement. 'Leave it to me,' was the answer that Mussolini sent back through my intermediary, 'I will mobilise the *mutilati* [disabled ex-soldiers] in Milan, and they will break the heads of any pacifists who try to hold anti-war meetings in the streets.' He was true to his word. The Fasci of the *mutilati*, the prototypes of the Fascisti who marched on Rome, made short work of the Milanese pacifists.[4]

Although the fascists had their strongest urban base in Milan, in the November 1919 elections Mussolini gained only 4,000 votes, compared with the 180,000 for the reformist Socialist Filippo Turati. In fact the fascists did not even get one MP elected. Not surprisingly, the editor of *Avanti!* wrote: 'There is a corpse in a state of putrefaction which has been fished out of the canal. We are talking about Benito Mussolini'.[5] The Socialists even led a mock funeral procession to his house, carrying a coffin – yet in a chilling example of how suddenly fascism can rise, three years later this 'corpse' would be prime minister and, shortly after, dictator of Italy.

For the time being, the Socialists were rampant. In their heartland of Emilia Romagna the PSI gained control of 223 out of 280 councils.[6] But despite these victories the PSI leadership had no analysis of how to go forward, of how to effectively create 'socialism'. This was another reason for the increasingly inevitable split between revolutionaries and reformists.

Mussolini did not fail to grasp that, despite its current strength, the Socialist Party could be beaten. Writing just three months after the PSI's massive election victory of November 1919, he commented:

They are impotent alike as reformers and revolutionaries. They take no action either in parliament or in the streets. The sight of a party wearing itself out on the morrow of a great victory in a vain search for something to apply its strength to, and willing to attempt neither reform nor revolution, amuses us. This is our vengeance, and it has come sooner than we hoped.[7]

The first major fascist attack on the left was an assault on the Milan office of *Avanti!*, the PSI daily, on 15 April 1919. A crowd of 300 assembled, armed with pistols, grenades and other weapons. The police stood aside and allowed the attack to go ahead, which led to the destruction of the offices and the death of three Socialists.[8] Not surprisingly Gramsci's newspaper, *Ordine Nuovo*, immediately felt the need to defend itself physically: barricades with barbed wire were placed behind the main street door, and the courtyard of the building was mined.

Some industrialists and members of the bourgeoisie quickly understood the usefulness of such a group, and began financing the fascists,[9] albeit at a relatively low level. For the period 1921-24 the breakdown of contributions to the Fascist Party has been calculated at 25 percent from individuals, 10 percent from banking and insurance, and 64 percent from industrialists and the business world at large.[10]

In their first phase, or 'wave', the fascists quickly became notorious for street fights with Socialists and arson attacks on their premises. However, urban fascism failed to grow significantly during 1919-20, and the PSI was still in the ascendant. But with the Socialists' inability to provide strong leadership or launch an insurrection, the more far-sighted fascists seized their chance to grow in the Po valley and Emilia after the occupation of the factories. What is extraordinary is that fascist advances occurred at the same time as Socialist election victories. As one author has argued:

> The [Socialist] party's electoral and membership growth was not paralleled by its ability to defend itself from armed gangs... Large-scale electoral success and widespread popular enthusiasm, therefore, were closely linked to the party's inability to deal with

the problem of open class conflict, which had been the subject
of a sterile debate over the previous two years.[11]

Unemployment began to grow in engineering, chemicals, construction, textiles and leather. Many factories put their workers
on a part-time basis. And as the industrial crisis deepened, and
emigration fell off, widespread unemployment started to spread
within agriculture. Wage rates declined, victimisations followed,
and strikes began to be defeated and became less frequent – for
example membership of the CGL union federation halved during
1921. While workers still voted for the left, they began to feel the
power of the boss again and, increasingly, the menace of the fascists.

One of the problems for the PSI was that it might have been
winning at the ballot box, but it did not in fact control the state,
which often stood by and allowed fascists to attack. One key
moment, representing the coming together of rural and urban
fascism, was the attack on the newly elected Socialist council in
Bologna on 21 November 1920. The new council was being
inaugurated that day, and the fascist attack led to 10 people being
murdered and 60 people being wounded.

Although this 'first wave' of fascism was smaller than the
second and third would be, it was nevertheless very bloody. During
the campaign for the April 1920 elections, 57 anti-fascists were
killed, a figure that rose to over 100 by 31 May.[12]

The second wave of fascism occurred in the countryside, and
was largely outside of Mussolini's control. Around towns such as
Ferrara the landowners' main crop, hemp, had fallen in value, and
to maintain their profits they had to drive down wages. Furthermore, peasants had been radicalised by the war, and in the South
they had begun to occupy land. Financed eagerly by large
landowners, the fascists systematically attacked the organising
centres of these structures. Fascists beat up Socialists, while
promising a return to traditional values and order. Unlike the
nationalist and populist fascism of the cities, rural fascism was
violently anti-Socialist and openly supported the interests of
large landowners. Mussolini wanted to be involved with this
second wave, and at the very beginning urged fascists on during

a rally in the town of Cremona: 'A million sheep will always be dispersed by the roar of a single lion'.[13]

But fascism always offered both a carrot and a stick to peasants. While it is not necessary to describe the 'persuasive power' of violence, fascists did talk about improving the economic situation of the peasantry – and in a situation where unemployment and poverty were rising, they rapidly gained a hearing. To the Socialist policy of collectivisation they counterposed the creation of large numbers of smallholdings through agreement with local landowners.[14] Gramsci admitted what was happening in *Ordine Nuovo* in July 1921:

> In Emilia, and the Veneto and Polesine regions, many peasant leagues have torn up their red flags and gone over to fascism…
> These leagues have been left to fend for themselves by national organisations – they have been told not to resist, to be cowardly, to passively accept all kinds of injustice and bullying. Scepticism has entered the hearts of these suffering, frightened and isolated masses – scepticism and demoralisation. What is the point of continuing to call yourself a Socialist and a revolutionary if all it means is that you get beaten up and shot, if socialism has fallen into the hands of indifferent men…who don't lift a finger to organise any kind of resistance and who don't attempt large-scale mobilisations against White tyranny?[15]

Overall Mussolini was alarmed by this second wave of rural fascism because it seemed too reactionary. At this stage he still preferred vague reactionary rhetoric without ever being very precise about his policies. Nevertheless, by mid-1921 many agricultural workers were abandoning the Socialists, and supporting agrarian fascism because of its promises. Yet the fascist movement was still relatively small – at the end of March official membership was 80,000, spread out over 317 branches. In big cities such as Milan fascism still had only 6,000 members, compared with medium-sized towns such as Ferrara with 7,000, or Cremona with 3,745.[16]

After this second phase in the countryside, which lasted from September 1920 to mid-1921, fascism experienced a third 'wave' of growth in urban areas from mid-1921 to October 1922. One of the key differences now was that ex-soldiers were far less noticeable – most of the active membership were petty-bourgeois youth and the long-term unemployed. For the latter, fascism sometimes represented a meal ticket. Many revolutionary syndicalists also left the movement, as they could see that it was by no means 'revolutionary'.

For industrialists, who had been wary of the fascists' radical rhetoric during their 'first wave', the success of rural fascism had shown that Mussolini was the right horse to back, and so they began financing fascism substantially in early 1921. Fascists were able to put Socialists and workers on the defensive in a way that the government had never been able to do. But the left's vote still held up very well in the May 1921 general election – the PSI gained 1,631,000 votes (compared with 1,835,000 in 1919), with the newly formed Italian Communist Party (PCI) receiving 305,000 votes.[17]

The PCI had been formed in January 1921 from a split at the Socialist Party congress in Livorno. In a card vote, 58,783 supported the motion put by Amadeo Bordiga, but these votes constituted a minority of the congress, so the communists walked out and announced the creation of a new party. The 15-man Central Committee accurately represented the various traditions of the membership: 'Five former abstentionists, seven maximalists, two from the *Ordine Nuovo*, and one from the Youth Federation'.[18] Yet this was a highly centralised party, and ultimate control lay with the five-man Executive Committee, essentially all 'absentionists' – followers of Bordiga.

Meanwhile fascist squads were now engaging in an orgy of violence. In the first six months of 1921 they destroyed 59 *case del popolo*, a key organising centre for the left. These premises literally embodied much of the history of the Italian workers' movement. First set up in Tuscany and Emilia in 1899, they were the meeting places of the local *Camere del lavoro* (trades councils), but each one was also used as a hiring hall and workers' labour exchange, club, educational centre and general head-quarters. It was due to their central role in organising both unions and members of the Socialist Party that fascists made them a central target in their rise to power. In the same period 119 separate trades council offices were ransacked, as were 107 cooperatives, 83 peasant union branches, 141 Communist and Socialist Party branches, 100 cultural centres and 28 union branches.[19]

The destruction of organising centres obviously meant the killing and wounding of many people. Ministry of the Interior statistics estimated that from the beginning of 1921 until 7 April 25 fascists and 41 Socialists were killed in political clashes. And in the two-week period of 16-31 May 16 fascists and 31 Socialists were killed.[20]

It was the very scale of these attacks that led to radical elements within the working class insisting upon a physical response to fascist squads. And the reason why this demand was raised so frequently was that the PSI, 'apart from numerous questions in parliament…did almost nothing to organise any military defence'.[21] A Socialist activist in the small Piedmont town of Monforte recalls a lively argument which at the same time reveals a sense of helplessness:

> One day in 1922 Romita [a PSI MP] came to give a speech and told us: 'Keep fighting.' ' "Keep fighting" my arse. It's you lot, the leadership, who have to keep fighting and give us some help – in any case, we hardly ever see you. Who are we meant to turn to tomorrow if we need help? To god? God has already lined up with the other lot'.[22]

Although anarchists did play a vital role within the movement generally, sadly some had a tendency to engage in individual 'deeds', or acts of terrorism. One notorious incident involved followers of the anarchist leader Errico Malatesta who wanted to kill a police chief in March 1921. The bombing attack went horribly wrong, perhaps through police infiltration, and 21 innocent people died in a theatre.[23]

Such acts of individual terrorism were completely different from the traditions of the organised working class (and, as we shall see, of the *Arditi del popolo* as well), ie open and mass resistance. This kind of terrorism is 'individual' not only in the sense that just a few individuals are involved in conspiring to launch the attack, but the person being targeted is also just one cog in a much larger wheel of capitalist domination. As Trotsky put it in 1911:

> The smoke from the explosion clears away, the panic disappears, the successor of the murdered minister makes his appearance, life again settles into the old rut, the wheel of capitalist exploitation turns as before – only police repression grows more savage and brazen. And as a result, in place of the kindled hopes and artificially aroused excitement come disillusion and apathy.[24]

Naturally enough, such actions were gifts for the authorities in terms of being able to clamp down on the left, as well as giving the fascists greater justification in their self-appointed task of keeping the left in line. (Echoes of this emerged again in Italy during the 1970s with the Red Brigades, whose limited but high-profile military actions aimed at substituting for a mass movement that was in decline.)

Fascism became an attractive proposition, whether for individuals terrified by terrorist attacks, or more importantly for factory owners fearful of the militancy of their workforce, and for liberal politicians terrified by the growth of socialism and communism. Indeed it was an attraction to many people in its early years due to its very vagueness – the only linking ideas were nationalism and patriotism. However, there came a point when fascism stopped being a movement and became the National Fascist Party (PNF) – on 9 November 1921. Its programme argued for a strong state, a right-wing economic policy, and an accommodating attitude towards the church. Although most early electoral support came from the lower middle class, once the PNF had solidified it quickly gained support from powerful industrialists and the ruling class in general.

The government miscalculated, believing fascism could be used as a battering ram against the PSI, and that Mussolini would become just another ordinary conservative politician. The fascists had run as joint candidates in Liberal politician Giovanni Giolitti's 'National Block' list in May 1921, which also included Nationalists, and gained just 35 seats out of over 500.

In an unguarded moment, Giolitti apparently once referred to the fascists as 'his Black and Tans'.[25]

But in fact it was the fascists who wanted to use Giolitti – indeed in July he was forced to resign as prime minister. At the opening ceremony of parliament fascist MPs showed their true colours, attacking and evicting from the chamber a PCI MP, Francesco Misiano, because he had deserted from the army. One MP commented: 'The Communists were the first. Then it was the turn of the Socialists, the Catholics, the Democrats and the Liberals. The last, unaware that their turn was to come, put themselves into the position of impartial judges, commenting on these events in very understanding tones'.[26] By now fascism had its own momentum – it virtually had its own private army, and the state rapidly conceded power. Indeed one author has argued: 'The two years prior to the March on Rome had witnessed a progressive abdication of the authority of the state in province after province, and its replacement with the authority of the fascists'.[27] It has been estimated that 100,000 rifles and muskets were passed from military arsenals to fascists during their rise to power.[28]

The reality was even worse: police forces would not only lend weapons to fascists, turning a blind eye to their attacks – they also fought alongside fascists in attacks on the left. Much of this had to do with the *biennio rosso* period, when the working class came dangerously close to seizing power. Ever since then the authorities had given the police far greater resources. The Royal Constabulary (which included the police) increased from 25,000 men in 1919 to 40,000 in 1921. The total number of *carabinieri* (a militarised police force that is part of the army) rose from 40,000 in 1919 to 75,000 in 1922.[29]

These kinds of forces could have easily curbed fascist violence – the reason fascists acted with impunity therefore had nothing to do with a lack of police resources, but had everything to do with political sympathy for them within the state. In essence the near-doubling of police manpower encouraged and contributed to fascist lawlessness in this period. For example a *carabiniere* colonel later wrote in his memoirs that in Tuscany '*carabinieri* and fascists were often side by side in a common struggle against the spread of anarchist subversion'.[30]

In February 1922 Bonomi resigned as prime minister, and after various negotiations Giolitti's right hand man, Luigi Facta, became prime minister in March. In July this government too collapsed, and Socialist leader Turati called for a coalition government made up of himself and Luigi Sturzo, leader of the Catholic-based Popular Party (PPI), which would restore legality and control the fascist squads, but nothing came of it. This was because most of the PSI was in a phase of ruling out any 'collaboration' with 'bourgeois governments', while the right of the PPI strongly opposed such an agreement too. Given the impossibility of such a solution, Facta became prime minister again.

By mid-1922 the fascists were becoming more and more audacious. In May fascist leader Italo Balbo mobilised between 40,000 and 63,000 unemployed agricultural workers in the Ferrara area, and occupied the city. The local economy had collapsed, and Balbo gave the authorities 48 hours to commit themselves to a massive expansion in public works programmes, otherwise he would take over the running of the town. After two days, with tens of thousands camped in the city streets, the authorities agreed to the fascists' demands.[31] Whereas before trade unions had played a vital role in allocating work to the unemployed, and negotiating pay and conditions at work, this role was now being taken over by fascists and their new 'corporate' trade unions.

Fascism was now dominant in the 'red belt' of central Italy – for example Bologna was occupied by 20,000 blackshirts for five days. In essence fascists now had physical control over whole towns and cities – only fascists could hold meetings, not the left. Control over public spaces had far more importance in this period, before television, radio and the internet. And, given that illiteracy was widespread, political argument was largely carried on face to face.

The anarchist leader Malatesta appealed to the entire left at the end of May:

Italy is facing the following dilemma – either a conscious working class will be able to radically weaken fascism, and with it the regime which supports it, or the majority of a more or less unaware population will allow, in the hope of a quiet life, an openly fascist government… It is high time to ask all progressive people – Socialists, Communists, Republicans and anarchists – not to renounce the beliefs to which they are all obliged to remain faithful, but to end their tantrums and personal animosities and work together in this hour of common danger, against a common enemy, in as much common action as possible.[32]

One last attempt to stem the tide was made by the trade union federations (in the form of an ad hoc *Alleanza del lavoro*, or Labour Alliance), which called for a 'legalitarian' general strike on 1 August, ie for 'the defence of political and trade union freedoms'.[33] But such were the conditions that the unions only decided to call the strike two days beforehand, and wanted the news to be kept secret until the day before. Furthermore, such were the divisions within the left, and its sectarianism (see following chapters), that preparations were rushed and half-hearted.

The strike was a failure. In the afternoon of the first day Sir Ronald Graham, British ambassador in Rome, sent a telegram to London: 'Strikers are being replaced by military and Fascisti. Almost full train service is running and telegraphs and telephones are not affected, and most of shops are open in Rome but newspapers have not appeared today'.[34]

The fascists seized their chance, and immediately stated they would launch reprisals and restore order if the strike did not end within 24 hours. In fact they mobilised immediately and, with the open support of the police and the army, attacked a strike that was clearly destined to failure: 'The fascist attack turns a failure into an out and out rout. The list of left-wing councils destroyed, and local branches and various organisations, spans the whole peninsula'.[35] The following list, which first quotes fascists' statistics and then other sources in brackets when available, estimates that in the first week of August: two (nine) *Case del popolo* were sacked, damaged or burnt down, 21 (25) trades councils, 16 PSI branches, 13 PCI branches (three anarchist branches), 11 (12) railway workers' union branches, 11 (13) co-operative movement branches (three seamen's union branches, two dockers' union branches, two unspecified union branches), five (eight) newspaper offices, and three (four) printing presses. Many flats and shops belonging to anti-fascists were also seriously damaged.[36]

In Genoa the big shipowners had set aside 1.5 million lire for a large-scale 'punitive expedition' against the city. In particular they wanted to break the direct labour scheme run by the dockers.[37] Barricades went up around the port, and railway workers stayed out on strike. The British consul-general, Frank Gibbs, commented that 'the Fascisti, who were organised on military lines, assisted the police in quelling the disturbances and as a matter of fact did most of the fighting themselves'.[38] Fighting raged for three days, until police armoured cars joined in the battle by opening fire with machine-guns, and thus tipping the balance of power.[39]

The fascists then occupied the dockers' headquarters and imposed a new dock labour scheme. The problem had been, the consul explained, that the dockers' scheme was 'killing all competition' by 'fixing their own tariffs which have always been prohibitive… Needless to say the commercial community expresses great satisfaction at this change of events'.[40] The following day it occurred to the consul that a victory for the Italian ruling class could also help the economic interests of the British ruling class: 'It is also a matter of interest to British shipowners, who will undoubtedly express their satisfaction at the turn of events'.[41] The working class in Genoa had been smashed: five people had been killed, over 50 wounded and more than 700 were arrested.

Back in London, the *Times* gloated: 'Fascismo has proved itself virile, well disciplined, fearless, and ready for emergencies. Certainly, the failure of the general strike is chiefly due to the ultimatum of the Fascisti threatening reprisals, and if Italian Socialism and democracy have now to suffer they have mainly themselves to blame'.[42]

In the context of a strike being doomed to failure, the fact that as part of their preparation Communist defence squads were instructed 'to cause maximum damage to our enemies and their property' shows just how ineffective PCI military organisation really was.[43] The PSI fared no better. Throughout 1921-22 the leadership had been in the hands of the 'maximalists', who insisted on no open involvement in bourgeois institutions whatsoever. This had become such an obsession that it was at a party congress just three weeks before Mussolini took power that the party expelled almost half its membership for the crime of 'collaborationism' with non-proletarian political forces.[44]

One of the most militant unions, the railway workers', which was also the union that had supported the *Arditi del popolo* the most, was now on the defensive too. Its branch in Rome reported that many of the members who had struck in the 'legalitarian' general strike had been sacked.[45] It turned out the sackings were themselves illegal, but such was the climate that no further strikes or activities were proposed to stem the tide. Membership of the CGL, the national union federation, had fallen to just 400,000 when Mussolini took power.

The above figures and events certainly make for depressing reading, but they should not be ignored – defeats hold vital lessons for the future. And one of the strongest points that needs to be stressed is that all of this might never have happened – if the *Arditi del popolo* had been supported by the rest of the left.

# Who were the Arditi del popolo?

All war veterans suffer some problems in readjusting to civilian life. But the psychological scars of combat were exacerbated by the economic problems of Italy after the First World War. At the end of 1918 soldiers came home to a country in severe economic crisis, with unemployment rising rapidly. Any savings or pensions that veterans had were quickly wiped out by high inflation.

Italian soldiers had been conscripted from all walks of life, and returned to a wide variety of social backgrounds and political influences. The roughly 40,000 ex-*Arditi* were an equally mixed group of people. The first organisation created for them, on 1 November 1919, the *Arditi* Association of Italy (AFAI), was clearly nationalist in its ideology, and was under the influence of both the Futurists and Mussolini's newspaper, *Il Popolo d'Italia*. In line with the ambiguous radicalism of early fascism, the founding statute of this organisation called for a 'regenerating revolution'. It also called for a minimum wage linked to a cost of living index, expropriation of inherited wealth above a certain level, distribution of uncultivated land to peasants, and workers' involvement in company management. But it also criticised those who 'stand against the fatherland', and stated its opposition against all forms of dictatorship, including those run by people with 'calloused hands'.[1] Yet the association was small, with probably under 1,000 members.[2]

It is important to stress the initially ambiguous nature of these ex-*Arditi*, which was the result both of their varied class position, and the efforts made by both Mussolini and left-wing parties to influence them – initially in the trenches, and then later as veterans.

So *Arditi*, as well as ordinary soldiers, were attracted by both political extremes in a polarised society. On one hand, it is clear that *Arditi* made up a sizeable number of the 120 people who founded the fascist movement in Milan in March 1919. And the following month about 40 *Arditi* took part in the first major fascist attack against the *Avanti!* offices described in the previous chapter. For much of the *biennio rosso* some *Arditi* groups were dubbed 'the White Guards of the Italian bosses'.

On the other hand, in an attempt to turn disaffected soldiers to the left, the Socialist Party set up a veterans' association named the Proletarian League at the end of 1918. Gramsci commented in the PSI daily *Avanti!* on 25 November:

> A new class consciousness has arisen, but not only in the factories –
> in the trenches as well, which have witnessed similar living condi-
> tions to those of the factory. This consciousness is raw – a clear level
> of political awareness has not yet been formed. It is raw material, yet
> to be worked upon. Our ideas must guide it. The working-class
> movement must absorb these masses, disciplining them and helping
> them to become aware of their own material and spiritual needs.
> It must educate every individual within it to provide total and
> permanent solidarity between one another.[3]

The League had some success in organising former soldiers, and as a result frequently suffered repression. One of the worst ex-amples was a police attack on a Sunday afternoon discussion in February 1920 in Milan, which left two dead and five injured.[4] Although the left was stronger in northern cities, the League also had a lot of success organising ex-soldiers in the South, who had expected the government to keep their promise of 'land to the peasants' once the war was over. It grew from a membership of 50,000 and 125 branches in April 1919 to a high point of 1 million ex-soldiers and 130,000 war widows in March 1920, organised in 896 branches. The divisions within the Socialist Party, as well as the appeal of nationalism and fascism, caused its rapid decline – in September 1921 it had been reduced to 30,000 members and fewer than 200 branches.[5]

Many Proletarian League branches were the backbone of what

became the first *Arditi del popolo* (ADP) groups. These groups arose spontaneously in the spring of 1921, and as one author says: 'Precisely because it did not have a party structure, this movement found support on the left… There was one single objective – to defeat fascism'.[6] In the port of Livorno there were armed defence squads organised against the fascists from as early as January 1921,[7] while in towns such as Ancona and Civitavecchia there was talk of an ADP branch as early as March and, during fighting in Parma the following month, the cry was heard 'Long live the *Arditi del popolo*'.[8]

In the same period in Turin there were groups calling themselves Red Guards, or in Genoa Red Wolves.[9] But the strength of the working class in Turin meant that the fascists launched relatively few attacks, thus reducing the need for the ADP to exist locally. Similarly in Milan, fascism had become quite moderate and parliamentary by 1921, again leading to very little ADP activity. In other words, lack of fascist activity in big cities was a consequence of their very weakness. But the sheer novelty of fascism made many people underestimate its danger. Looking back many years later, the anarchist leader Armando Borghi recalled: 'Each time the fascists concentrated their forces in just a few places. Once they had destroyed one area, they went on to another. They isolated the areas they were most afraid of from the rest of the country, and sorted them out at the end. Those who hadn't yet been attacked didn't see all this – they couldn't understand'.[10]

The town of Genzano, just outside Rome, seemed particularly well organised in May 1921, with 200 members who apparently had 30 rifles, 200 pistols and 200 hand grenades, all of which became part of the ADP upon its foundation. The leadership group was composed of six Communists and an anarchist.[11]

Essentially, after more than a year of widespread fascist attacks, working-class activists were instinctively pushed into organising the kind of unitary resistance their leaders were unwilling to set up. This resistance was born out of necessity rather than any macho posturing. In essence it was a collective form of self-preservation.

Such was the growth in this urge for self-preservation that 10 days before the birth of the ADP, 800 left-wing activists met in

Rome and passed a motion stating: 'It is necessary to create immediate acts of proletarian defence, which challenge the disruptive and repressive actions of bourgeois and monarchic madness throughout Italy'.[12] The ADP were a necessary response to a rapidly changing situation – the decline in mass working-class mobilisations following the occupation of the factories had encouraged the growth of fascism. The growth in fascist violence in turn then necessitated some form of defence.

The ADP proper emerged from within the Roman branch of another *Arditi* grouping, the National Association of *Arditi*, or ANAI, in late June 1921, and was formed to specifically counter the attacks of fascist squads.[13] Yet its creation was a microcosm of what was happening in Italy as a whole – the existing ANAI branch had been inactive for more than a year, partly due to passivity and partly due to deep-set political differences. One side of the divide was led by Giuseppe Bottai, a fascist MP and later minister in Mussolini's government, while the other was led by Lieutenant Argo Secondari. Taking advantage of the branch's inactivity, Secondari called a meeting of about 100 people on 22 June to form a new organisation, the ADP. A police spy reported: 'In that meeting and in those which followed Secondari explained that the programme was that of fighting fascism and, through strong organisation, defending and looking after working-class parties, premises and branches against the violence and outrages of the enemy'.[14] Meetings quickly followed in other cities: Cremona, Livorno, Parma and Pisa. Significantly, these organisations generally met in *Case del popolo*, trades-council or Proletarian League premises.

Secondari was a very representative figure of the ADP as a whole. He had come back from America to volunteer for military service in the First World War. Enrolling as a private, he was promoted to lieutenant and was awarded a bronze medal. He may also have briefly taken part in the nationalist occupation of Fiume. Politically, up until the creation of the ADP he could be said to be a follower of D'Annunzio, with anarchist and republican leanings. He became directly involved in political activity in July 1919, during a wave of strikes and looting in Rome against high food prices. Soldiers were being used to guard shops and government buildings, so Secondari and other *Arditi* went to the Pietralata barracks and attempted to win them over by argument, also with a view to obtaining weapons. It's likely that the weapons were to be used to control the major food markets and guarantee free food distribution. The attempt failed and Secondari was later arrested. However, this whole episode later got distorted and PCI and PSI leaders, knowingly or unknowingly, presented it as some kind of attempt to launch a military coup.[15]

Regardless of the figure of Secondari, the ADP were far clearer than the rest of the left on what to do, perhaps because they had one limited aim – to stop fascist attacks, with violence if necessary. As Secondari responded to fascist objections during an early meeting of the ADP: 'A river of blood and smoking ruins separate fascists and *Arditi*'.[16] In a spontaneously born movement, political allegiances were a secondary matter compared to the urgent task of organising resistance. So Guido Picelli, a Socialist Party member, led the movement in Parma, PCI member Francesco Leone in Vercelli, and so on. Other groups existed throughout Italy – in Collegno, Crema, Livorno, Naples, Orte, Ravenna and Vicenza.

The movement's first manifesto, published on 30 June, is a good illustration of the contradictory past of *Arditi* members. On the one hand they had decided to break with fascism and oppose it, while on the other they were still influenced by the ideas of D'Annunzio and therefore nationalism:

> The old system is collapsing and it needs to be brought crashing to the ground. In any event, workers have irrevocably decided not to be intimidated any more. They have called upon us to represent them and we greeted their request enthusiastically… We never sold or prostituted ourselves. An anarchic formation *par excellence*, we were uncontaminated by the germs of passionate imperialism… We are subversives in the broadest sense of the word, we will never sell ourselves to tyranny, we will not be distracted by goals which are not our own… We reject the manipulations and greed of patriotism, which takes pride only in its race. We avoid all nationalist scheming.[17]

The creation of the *Arditi* was just one example of the working class rapidly trying to come to terms with the need to organise physical resistance to fascist squads. A meeting held at the same time as the issuing of the first manifesto illustrated another feature of the anti-fascist movement – an ad hoc 'Roman proletarian defence committee' met and called for a demonstration on 6 July. Two representatives attended from the Roman trades council, as well as members of the Republican Party and individuals who defined themselves as anarcho-communists. Nobody attended from the Communist or Socialist parties.

Events were now moving rapidly. On 2 July a meeting of 300 *Arditi* was held in Rome. Donations were pouring in: in a matter of days 15,000 lire was collected, mainly from railwaymen, builders and post office workers.[18]

And on 6 July 1921 3,000 *Arditi* met for their first and last national rally at the Botanical Gardens in Rome, with sizeable delegations coming from Emilia Romagna, Lazio and Campania. Argo Secondari was by now unquestionably the leader, with another major activist being Umberto Beer from Ancona, a D'Annunzio sympathiser.[19] Their message was simple – they were a military organisation formed to defeat fascist violence. But this was far from being a small group engaging in individual acts of terrorism against fascists. It was a movement that had the potential to become very big, and which organised public events and published a newspaper sporadically.

The rally had also been publicised in the press (although the Socialist daily *Avanti!* refused to print the advert), and was called as part of a national demonstration against fascist violence. The manifesto for the demonstration demanded that fascists be disarmed and that their organisation be outlawed. It went on to say that it never expected these demands to be met 'because it has been the authorities themselves who have encouraged the creation of a fascist movement, financing it, arming it, and protecting it at every turn'.[20]

The Rome trades council, and the PSI, PCI, PRI (Italian Republican Party) and other left-wing organisations subsequently called for a general strike in the afternoon, in order for people to go to the demonstration. *L'emancipazione*, a weekly Socialist paper, estimated that more than 50,000 attended, and described the start of the march thus: 'Receiving great applause and admiration, the *Arditi del popolo* made their first appearance, formed up in three battalions of a thousand men each, waving their flags'.[21]

The Roman police were very nervous – 800 men, two armoured cars and four machine-guns were placed inside the Colosseum. Many *carabinieri* guarded the armoury, and cavalry patrolled the open space around the Colosseum to prevent a large crowd from gathering. Nevertheless, the crowd was singing *Bandiera Rossa* when a huge cheer went up as the *Arditi* arrived, marching in military formation, each carrying 'roughly hewn clubs'. As one of the speakers, Nicola Bombacci, took to the stage he was greeted with shouts of 'Viva Russia! Viva Communism!' – perhaps because he had been a delegate to the Third International congress the year before. Bombacci noted that there were many flags representing many different ideas, but said they all came together in a single army with a sole purpose: 'Moving towards their own liberation'.[22]

Two days later the Rome chief of police wrote in a report that the size and nature of the demonstration 'shocked the leaders of the local fascist movement, who began to worry about the new situation emerging within the Roman working class'. What was more interesting was the fact that 'membership has risen to 800, but many more applications are arriving, especially after the organisation's show of strength at the Botanical Gardens rally of 6 July'.[23]

On 9 July the *Arditi* organised a meeting of 600 people, in which those who didn't have an ADP badge were given one. It was also announced that the local railway workers' branch had offered a donation of £140, and that appeal sheets to use in union branches were available.[24] Such an enthusiastic response from workers proved that the ADP were fulfilling a need. The following day the *Arditi* held their own public rally, where membership cards were available for people who came from outside Rome. Secondari gave the main speech, and according to the police it included the promise that the ADP 'will do what the revolutionary parties have so far been unable to do'.[25] The following day, 11 July, the minister of the interior saw fit to tell local police chiefs of the existence of the ADP, warning them that they had emerged from 'the most dis- turbing elements of anarchy, republicanism and socialism, with the intention of violent opposition to fascist activities'.[26]

The attitude of the authorities also pushed the ADP into the heart of the working class. Once they were evicted from their first headquarters in central Rome, they subsequently held their meet- ings at a *Casa del popolo*, or at the offices of the bakers' union or the anarchist print union.[27] On 25 July 60 *Arditi* delegates met at the Rome trades council building, in a booking organised by the tram workers' union – it was their first and last congress. One of the main points made in a motion presented by Secondari was that he did not want political factions within the organisation. The problem wasn't that new ADP members had party membership cards in their pock- ets or sold their papers at meetings. The issue was that any ADP member would have to automatically accept that they would sometimes be organised on the basis of military discipline.[28]

The reason why this motion was the central item for discussion was because many individuals, particularly Communists, were torn between their desire to be part of the ADP but at the same time felt an allegiance to party discipline. The tragedy is that such a difficulty could have been easily resolved if the party hadn't had such a rigid sense of discipline, and accepted that under certain conditions members could act with a degree of freedom as mem- bers of other organisations, normally those with 'narrower' aims than a party. (The Communist International in Moscow, under the leadership of Trotsky and Lenin, was beginning to grapple with such an issue at the time, which became known as the 'united front' policy, but clarification came just too late in the Italian situation – although it is unclear whether the PCI leadership in 1921 would have accepted such a policy in any event. These issues are discussed in greater detail in the chapter entitled 'Why the left failed to fight'.)

According to police reports, Secondari also asked delegates to find out precise details of road and rail transport in their area, in order to be able to move quickly to oppose fascist attacks. He also insisted that members get hold of guns.[29] A 'Programme of Action' was also passed.[30] Although Secondari and Beer were the two main leaders elected in Rome, the appointment of PSI MP Giuseppe Mingrino and Republican Vincenzo Baldazzi to the leadership group soon afterwards gave it a broader political base.

At the end of the congress fighting broke out with the police, which lasted throughout the night. A policeman was killed, and initially the *Arditi* were accused, although it later turned out he was killed by drunken hooligans. Secondari and other *Arditi* were arrested.

The congress claimed the organisation already had 154 branches and 55,000 members, although this was almost certainly an exaggeration.[31] On the other hand police reports during the summer of 1921 – the high point of ADP activity – stated that ADP groups were active in 56 out of 71 provinces. The most detailed analysis made by a historian recently estimated a membership of 20,000 divided up into 144 branches.[32] Nevertheless, by September the ADP had a membership structure, including cards and badges.

The nature of ADP activity also needs to be stressed. Their basic drive was to involve the largest number of people possible in resisting fascism, so in many ways membership levels should be seen as the tip of an active anti-fascist iceberg. One of the ways they got themselves noticed was by organising marches through working-class areas. This influence could be seen in Rome at the end of July. Following yet another fascist outrage in a town outside the capital, a general strike was called in Rome and the entire Lazio region. The significance of this was that the ADP had asked the trades council to call it, and the unions had agreed.[33] The strike itself was a partial success, mainly because the authorities banned all marches and rallies. But more importantly the fascists did not try to intervene against it.[34]

Gramsci and the *Ordine Nuovo* newspaper quickly took a positive line towards the ADP. A long interview with Secondari was published on 12 July, in which he argued: 'Today it is no longer appropriate to talk about left-wing violence. The sad monopoly of political banditry is held solely by the fascists. And if the *Arditi* were not to intervene in the face of the fascists' systematic war against the Italian proletariat and its institutions, they would be betraying themselves'.[35] Gramsci then followed this up on 15 July with his own personal appraisal, showing a clear understanding of the dangers:

> It is essential to make [the working class] understand what they were not made to understand in September 1920 – when the working people leave the terrain of legality but do not find the necessary spirit of sacrifice and political capacity to carry their actions through to the end, they are punished by mass shootings, by hunger, by cold, by inactivity which kills slowly, day by day.[36]

This is why he called for Communists to support the ADP, because 'they want the arming of the proletariat, the creation of an armed proletarian force which is capable of defeating the bourgeoisie'. Gramsci was now one of the few leaders of the left who was beginning to develop an accurate understanding of the nature of fascism. In this key article he pointed out that 'it is essential to compel them to understand that today the proletariat is confronted not just by a private organisation, but by the whole state apparatus, with its police, its courts, its newspapers which manipulate public opinion as the government and capitalists please'.[37]

In conclusion, the potential of the ADP can be seen from the fact that its membership came from many different political traditions. The majority were probably Communists, but there were also many anarchists, Republicans, Socialists, revolutionary syndicalists – and even some Catholics. Socially the organisation was predominantly working class, with a very high proportion of railway workers.[38]

But the ADP was born at a very difficult time – exactly when the Socialists and fascists signed a 'peace pact', part of which obliged the PSI leadership to disown the ADP, which they immediately did – something that will be discussed in the next chapter. This is why the ADP's major strength was at a local level – national organisations snubbed them, and defensive actions tended to develop very quickly from area to area.

# Stopping fascism

## Sarzana and the crisis of fascism

One of the first major acts of resistance by the ADP was organised in the Socialist-run town of Sarzana, on the Ligurian-Tuscan border. According to one writer, the fascists' defeat at Sarzana 'made Mussolini think twice and led him to practise greater caution. In fact he became devious, and tried to hide fascism's violent side, and also started talking repeatedly about alliances and peace pacts'.[1]

On 17 July 1921 local ADP members, organised by two ex-*Arditi* lieutenants, Silvio Delfini and Papiro Isopo, clashed with three lorryloads of fascists on the edge of town. One fascist was killed. The following day fascists from Carrara again tried to enter the town, and again the ADP blocked them. This time 10 fascists were arrested.[2]

The town the fascists were attacking was particularly radical. Many inhabitants had worked, or continued to work, in the nearby weapons factories of La Spezia or the traditionally anarchist stronghold of Carrara. In fact, the day after the first fascist attack a general strike had taken place in the town, and lookouts were posted on the outskirts.[3]

Local fascist leaders Amerigo Dumini and Tullio Tamburini (the former murdered PSI MP Giacomo Matteotti in 1924, while Tamburini was founder of the Florentine *fascio*) announced they were about to launch a 'punitive expedition' against the town, an announcement that gave the ADP precious time to organise.[4]

The fascist attack came at dawn on 21 July, as 600 to 1,000 blackshirts arrived in Sarzana by train. However, the town had already been alerted to their presence by some railway workers, whose train had been fired upon.[5] Discussions ensued between the fascists and the police in the square outside the station, with the fascists demanding the right to march through the town and the immediate release of the fascists under arrest. But they quickly became outraged and impatient at the police's respect for legal niceties, and opened fire on them. However, the superior military skills of the police quickly caused a rout in the fascist ranks, and the majority of fascists were holed up in the station for several hours until they were allowed to leave. Over 100 fascists tried to make a break for it through the fields, but they were intercepted by armed ADP members, and peasants with pitchforks and scythes,[6] who probably killed seven by hanging them from trees or drowning them in ditches. The fascists were put on trains to get them out of town, and they were then shot at by ADP members from concealed positions. The fascists suffered 18 dead and 30 wounded.[7]

One of the main fascist leaders of the Sarzana attack later admitted that the fascists were not prepared to engage in a real battle. Up until that point: 'Fascism has not found itself facing people prepared to stand their ground... The squads are too used to winning against an enemy that nearly always runs away or reacts weakly. They didn't know how, and were therefore incapable of dealing with this'.[8]

The fascist movement experienced a real crisis at this point. The more 'intransigent' elements launched even more violent actions – two Communists were killed in Carrara, and large fascist demonstrations were quickly organised in Bologna and Padua.[9]

Mussolini, however, moved in the opposite direction. He was concerned that a series of defeats could seriously undermine the morale of the blackshirts. And he moved very fast – the fascist national council assembled for an emergency meeting the same evening the news came through from Sarzana. A long debate followed and, eventually, Mussolini won the vote 21 to five, in support of trying to reach a 'peace' agreement with the Socialists.

Mussolini quickly stated in parliament that he wanted to hold out an 'olive branch' to the left. The PSI and trade union leaders leapt at the chance, because even before the battles in Sarzana they had been negotiating a 'peace pact' with the fascists. On 31 July *Avanti!* criticised the ADP. Deliberately ignoring the nature of what had happened at Sarzana, they took a very defeatist position just a few days before the signing of the pact: 'The passionate and sentimental ADP are obviously deluding themselves over the possibility of stopping an armed movement of reaction when it is protected and helped by the state'.[10] While allowing for the fact that the paper was preparing the ground for the public signing of the pact, what clearly underlies such a concept is the belief that 'public order', or in this instance the defence of working-class communities, can only be left to the forces of the state, even if they are in league with fascists.

The pact was finally signed on 3 August. The main political consequence was the political isolation of the ADP, given that point six of the agreement stated: 'The Socialist Party declares itself to be unconnected to the organisation *Arditi del popolo* and its activities'.[11]

But the PSI did not universally agree to the pact. *Avanti!* commented: 'We are not satisfied with this truce. It does not mean peace, because there can't be peace between the persecuted and the persecutor.' Two socialist leaders in Milan responded by declaring their support for the ADP. On a national level Giacinto Serrati's grouping within the PSI, which was to the left of Turati, were particularly hostile to the pact.

At the same time as Socialist dissent surfaced over the peace pact, so too did fascist dissent. Two fascist leaders resigned, including one of the top five national leaders, Roberto Farinacci. The other leader, Piero Marsich, immediately wrote an article in his local fascist newspaper entitled 'Peace Isn't Made by Signing Treaties but by Changing Governments'. And his local association, in the Veneto region, passed a motion against the peace process.[12]

Another major leader, Dino Grandi, could not have made his disagreement with Mussolini any plainer in a newspaper editorial: 'Gentlemen, let's stop messing about! If we need something today, it's not a ridiculous peace pact, but rather a gradual and solid military preparation for our revolutionary future – against the socialist state which is inevitably being prepared'.[13] A meeting of 400 fascists in Florence passed a motion stating they had 'no faith in the so-called peace negotiations which, even if completed, would come into conflict with the irresistible course of events –

the contempt of the official Socialist Party, and the anti-Italian spirit and actions of the Communist Party'.[14]

The clash within fascism concerned the most fundamental aspects of its existence – the nature of the movement in the future and how it hoped to come to power. Not for nothing did Mussolini write at the time: 'The month of July 1921 is a fatal one in the history of Italian fascism'.[15]

The 'extremist' wing of fascism, often based in small central Italian towns, had built itself up thanks to the services it provided for local landowners – essentially repressing working-class radicalism. Any real 'peace pact' would mean an end to their role, and by implication the evolution of fascism into a much more 'moderate' and 'political' movement. The extremists argued for some vague kind of 'revolution' in order to gain power. Dino Grandi defined the peace pact as 'a vulgar little trap', while Mussolini's majority wanted to negotiate their way into office.

Such was the scale of conflict that Mussolini could only go for broke. The same day he signed the pact he openly criticised those fascist leaders who:

> …lock themselves in and become blind, and who don't believe in the existence of a much bigger, complex and difficult world… Those who are unable to develop such a synthesis can have the right attributes to lead a squad of 20 men, but they certainly can't demand the privilege to lead vast masses of people in the most turbulent moments of their history.

And the following day he warned that the Socialists would score a victory if the fascists didn't respect the peace pact: 'Their victory doesn't lie in the peace treaty, but in this lack of discipline, this terrifying blindness which is about to lose us a section of Italian fascism'.[16]

The point Mussolini was trying to get across was that fascism had neither the military strength nor the political support to seize power directly. Any head-on clash could well lead to a crushing defeat for the movement:

> Don't people realise that fascism has become synonymous with terror among the non-Socialist population as well? I broke this

chain of events. I opened a gap in the barbed wire of hate – this
unstoppable frustration of vast popular masses that would have
swept you away. I have opened up many possibilities for fascism
again. Could fascism exist without me? Certainly. But I can also
exist without fascism. There's room for everyone in Italy, even
for 30 fascisms. But this would mean no fascism.[17]

The dissidents continued to disagree over the next few days and
on 18 August, two weeks after signing the peace pact, Mussolini
resigned as leader. Fascism was leaderless and divided. The crisis
continued throughout the summer, with local fascist squads
launching frequent attacks against the left.

Both sides of fascism came to realise that they could not do
without each other. Slowly the notion that fascism needed to
become a unified national party started to predominate. The violence continued, but in the long term 'politics' would prevail.

Yet the very existence of the peace pact meant that the PSI had
disarmed itself politically, although on the ground its membership
continued stubborn resistance. The PSI had effectively tied both
hands behind its back, and the real tragedy is that the PCI more
or less did the same, but in a different way.

By mid-July Gramsci had shifted significantly from his previous
position of underestimating fascism and being relatively unin-
terested in anti-fascist work. On 21 July he wrote: 'It is up to the
local forces to give thought to their own defence. Viterbo and
Sarzana have given the example of what must be done'.[18]

But although Gramsci was a major leader of the PCI, he was
not the dominant one. On 10 July, four days after the ADP rally
at Rome's Botanical Gardens, Bordiga told the Rome branch
that the party needed to take a position on the ADP nationally,
and that until that happened branch members had to curb their
enthusiasm for working with the ADP.[19]

And despite the fascists' clear defeat in Sarzana, the PCI leadership were to quickly take an openly hostile stance against the
ADP. While Gramsci and the *Ordine Nuovo* group supported
their actions, at the same time several articles in Amadeo Bordiga's
*Il Comunista* criticised them. The first major article was published

on 14 July, and showed how the PCI was unwilling to work with any other organisation: 'The proletariat's revolutionary military organisation must be on a *party* basis, closely linked to the party's network of political organisms. Communists therefore cannot and must not take part in activities organised by other parties, or which in any event arise outside the party.'

Plans were then announced for the creation of Communist squads, in direct competition with the ADP. As one communique spelt out: 'Nobody who is a member of the party or the youth federation can belong to similar organisations'.[20]

However, these squads were slow to come into life and, in any event, ADP formations were already in existence, or rather were coming into life in towns where there was a non-sectarian tradition on the left. For example, the 23 year old Giuseppe Alberganti moved to the small Lombardy town of Arona when he was appointed as a train driver, and later recalled:

> I took on the job of [PCI] branch secretary, either immediately before or at the same time as the creation of the *Arditi del popolo*. But I had already been leading anti-fascist activities, so it was easy to develop our anti-terrorist action, calling ourselves the *Arditi del popolo*. The important thing wasn't the name we gave it, but the fact that it created a mass movement, far bigger than those groups which were clearly defined as Communist.[21]

Given the urgency of the situation, many PCI members used their common sense and joined the ADP. Consequently a leadership document published at the end of July complained: 'Many members and some party organisations insist on proposing, or sometimes initiating, Communist involvement in organisations which are outside our party, such as the *Arditi del popolo*.' Strangely, these members were criticised for 'letting themselves be led by emotional and romantic considerations', yet at the same time the leadership commented of the ADP: 'Their apparent greater popularity will not distract us from our specific task.' The fundamental problem for the PCI leadership was the very purpose of the ADP: 'Organising the proletariat's reaction to the excesses of fascism, with the aim of re-establishing "order and normality in social life". The aim of Communists is very different – they want to lead proletarian struggle until a revolutionary victory'.[22]

Returning to the local level, a local Bordigist MP visited the branch secretary in Arona, but young Alberganti stood his ground: 'I told him, without a clear and committed leadership the fascists would beat us. The fact that the *Arditi del popolo* had the support of anti-fascists, who were in turn in a big majority among the working class, meant that for a Communist the best thing was to stay linked to the masses'.[23]

Despite this kind of feedback from below, the PCI Executive Committee dug its heels in at a meeting on 7 August. One of the reasons Bordiga gave for his hostility was that ADP leaders such as Argo Secondari were 'ambiguous', and that fifth columnists could have entered the organisation with some kind of strategic intent. The 'strongest measures' would be taken against any members who joined the ADP. Incredibly, many of the suspicions voiced by PCI leaders came from fascist sources, who had started spreading rumours that the *Arditi* were backed by the government and were acting, ultimately, in its defence.[24]

Despite the leadership's position, *Ordine Nuovo* continued to comment positively on the ADP and publish details of their meetings. And on the ground many Communists, particularly young ones, had strong reservations about the PCI's stance. Four months after the leadership's insistence that PCI members take no part in ADP activities, the party leader responsible for military work complained: 'It is deplorable that in many provinces Communists are still mistaken with the so-called *Arditi del popolo*. This must not continue'.[25]

The disowning of the ADP by the PSI and PCI leaderships left the group exposed to attacks by the government and fascists. In early August *Arditi* in several cities were charged with the serious offence of belonging to a subversive organisation. And on 17 August prime minister Ivanoe Bonomi (an ex-Socialist) wrote to the justice minister asking him to harass the ADP, resulting in a circular being sent out to investigating magistrates and appeal court judges on 5 September. Bonomi had already written to prefects and police chiefs on 13 August asking them to arrest anyone involved in military-style parades, and to seize any weapons used in them.[26]

These actions contrast with the government's refusal to take any significant action against fascist squads during the previous two years. But Bonomi's hostility to the ADP shouldn't be surprising – after all, he had been elected on a joint ticket with the fascist party, and on more than one occasion he allowed fascists to borrow his ministerial car in order to carry out their 'punitive expeditions'.[27]

Another repressive manoeuvre was to ban the ADP from collecting any money in public, and to seize any money collected, often through the excuse of not having a public licence to do so. Not only was money required to buy weapons, it was also needed for publicity, legal fees, and assistance for the hundreds of people who had been arrested. This was an attempt to cut off the very lifeblood of the movement.[28]

It was in this context that another manifesto was published by the ADP in the left-wing press, on 28 August. It began by saying: 'We came from nothing, into a hellish struggle.' Compared with earlier manifestos this was far more sophisticated analytically, stating: 'Fascists have been organising crimes for three years. Powerful in terms of resources and weapons, supported by the authorities, with the consent of the government, unpunished in their actions, they could never be defeated in a single day. And unfortunately many areas are still suffering bloodshed.' But the manifesto pointed out that in towns such as Sarzana 'the bells rang out, the call for a fightback was heard, and the *Arditi* answered the call like lightning… Freedom has returned. Threats and aggression have ended.' The ADP were clearly aware of the consequences of the signing of the peace pact: 'Just as the government's reaction is being unleashed against us, the political parties, the very parties that represent you – O workers – fall silent'.[29]

As regards fascist action, at 10am on 31 October fascists burst into Argo Secondari's house in Rome, wounding him in the head and causing him to have concussion.[30]

The ADP were now a long way from the 'July days' of Sarzana, of the Rome rally and mass meeting. They were politically isolated – unable to grow both politically and numerically in any real sense. But despite all this they still managed to put up significant resistance over the coming year, simply because many working-class communities were not prepared to just turn the other cheek to fascist attacks.

# The first March on Rome

The third fascist national congress was called in Rome in November. Mussolini intended it to be a clear demonstration of the strength of his movement and, with 35,000 blackshirts mobilised and starting to arrive in Rome, acts of violence were inevitable. To facilitate their arrival the Ministry of Public Works had even agreed that railway passengers heading to Rome wearing fascist party badges could travel free.[31]

In essence, the fascists wanted to do in Rome what they had been doing in many other cities, and the first contingents behaved in the normal way: 'Walking through the streets, the fascists thought they could treat the working people of the capital in the same way they had treated workers and peasants in the provinces. They started ripping off badges and red handkerchiefs, and beating people up'.[32]

In anticipation of these events, on 7 November the Roman leadership of the ADP had issued the following warning:

> Given that in recent days squads of fascists, armed with revolvers, clubs and iron bars, are harassing citizens and carrying out acts of violence against people and property, we are unfortunately obliged to deny all responsibility in being able to control the correct and sacrosanct protests of the Roman proletariat.[33]

Anticipating a decisive clash, the ADP leadership called on their numerous membership from the surrounding Lazio region to come to the city.

Guerrilla warfare was to rage in Rome from 9 to 13 November, culminating in the fascists' defeat and withdrawal. The spark was the murder of a railway worker on 9 November. The first train carrying 600 fascists arrived at San Lorenzo station in Rome at 7.30am, and the fascists celebrated by firing 100 shots into the shunting yards. Although nobody was killed or wounded, the word spread to local factories, and many workers walked out and congregated on the railway lines, forcing the next train full of 700 fascists, due to arrive at 8.45am, to stop. The police quickly arrived and managed to get the train moving again, but as it pulled away a shot was fired from the last carriage, and a railway worker was killed.[34]

A general strike then began to spread spontaneously, called by the 'Proletarian Defence Committee', although it was later made official. Three organisations officially belonged to the committee – the two Roman trades councils and the Republican Party. Many individual anarchists and *Arditi* went to the meetings, as did Communist trade unionists, particularly railway workers. The Socialist Party was not closely involved, as it was worried about the use of working-class violence, preferring to concentrate on calls for the authorities to disarm the fascists. In any event, some offensive attacks were made on fascist columns, although most occurred on the edge of the city because railway workers had stopped the trains on the outskirts, thus leaving many fascists isolated from their main forces.[35]

Clashes took place throughout the day between fascists, anti-fascists and the 'forces of law and order', and by the end of the day four people were dead and 150 wounded. The fascists managed to hold their national march in the city centre, estimated at 10,000. Meeting in congress, they warned that if calm wasn't restored to the city they would take care of it themselves.[36]

By the morning of 10 November most fascists had managed to come together in the city centre. They found themselves in a city with no newspapers, transport, postal services or bakeries. The Proletarian Defence Committee renewed its strike call in a manifesto distributed at midday:

> The anti-fascist strike is continuing in a compact and disciplined fashion. Yesterday all fascist attempts to attack working-class areas were promptly repulsed by workers. Work will resume when all fascists, who have come to Rome clearly aiming at provocation, go back to their home towns – where we hope our fellow workers will use your huge mobilisation as an example of how to win.[37]

Partly due to the feeling of being surrounded, and partly due to their desire to show their strength, fascist columns continued to attack the inner-city working-class suburbs of San Lorenzo, Testaccio, Tiburtino, Trastevere and Trionfale. However, armed lookouts had been placed on the main approach roads, and women were ready on the roofs and at windows with stones, flowerpots and tiles.[38] Repeated attacks took place, with police connivance, but they were all repulsed. A total of five fascists and seven *Arditi* were killed, with over 200 wounded, including a fascist MP.[39] Small groups of fascists continued to march round the city centre with their flags, beating up anyone who didn't show them full respect – such as a pregnant woman who was kicked in the stomach and suffered a miscarriage, and an armless war veteran attacked for not taking his cap off.[40] Arguments continued to rage within the Proletarian Defence Committee, which on Friday evening had temporarily voted to lift the strike – a vote that was overturned by the arguments put forward by Communist railway workers.[41]

As for the fascists, due to their failure to subdue the opposition Mussolini was forced to order those attending the congress not to leave the hotel where it was taking place. An MP warned them to bring the congress to an end quickly 'to avoid more serious reprisals from local people'.[42] The remaining fascists wanted to leave, but the problem they had now was that railway workers were on strike, so government ministers had to plead with union leaders to put on special trains.

As the fascist congress ended, the working class understood it had defended its territory, buildings and printing presses. Tens of thousands of armed fascists had come to Rome, and were essentially allowed a free rein by the police, yet trade union and Socialist Party leaders effectively fell silent in those crucial hours, saying nothing and organising nothing. Apart from the heroic military resistance, what had disoriented the fascists and worried the government was the indefinite strike – which showed no signs of stopping until the fascist squads left the capital.

In the meantime Mussolini was escorted to the station by two armoured cars provided by the government, and the following day, when the bulk of the fascists left, they too had to be escorted out of the city by the police.[43] In frustration, they wrecked their congress venue, the Augusteo theatre.

Politically, however, the fascists had used the Rome congress to turn themselves from a movement into a party, the National Fascist Party (PNF). In the long term it was political developments such as this which carried more weight with the ruling class, rather than a military victory by anti-fascists.

There was another worrying fact to note from the anti-fascist victory in Rome – the lack of PCI involvement. One dissident Communist, Vittorio Ambrosini, recalled: 'The PCI was almost totally detached from the movement in Rome... In an article our party's official newspaper...repeated the same old story about the movement's lack of purity'.[44]

Gramsci's *Ordine Nuovo* put forward quite a different but slightly odd analysis. On one hand it applauded the creation of a united front in Rome, but it also criticised 'the petty-bourgeois nature of the action against fascism, aimed at re-establishing the rule of law... The people of Rome did not fight a class war with their strike call'.[45] People such as Gramsci had still not fully understood the growing strength of the fascist movement, and even at this crucial stage were unwilling to fully recognise that, compared with the near-revolutionary situation of September 1920 just 10 months earlier, the working class was now on the defensive and needed allies. This meant creating alliances on the ground, even outside of the working class. Instead Gramsci's newspaper was full of articles viciously attacking the middle classes – many of whom, as the paper acknowledged, had actually taken an active part in opposing the fascist invasion of Rome. Not only did these people hate the violence and arrogance of fascists, they would be wondering why the government allowed the fascists to march in Rome, while simultaneously banning a march by young Catholics. And why did the fascists gratuitously destroy one of the city's major theatres?

The importance of the middle classes is that throughout history they have always lined up with either the forces of reaction or the forces of revolution. At times of profound conflict the middle classes are obliged to choose between the ruling class and the working class. The tragedy in Italy over the next year was that the fascists managed to win over the urban middle classes – and part of the reason for this was that much of the left was sectarian, obsessed with attacking the middle classes as a whole rather than winning large sections of them to an anti-fascist position.

# Parma bell'arma[1]

The final successful act of resistance by the ADP was in the city of Parma, and it was the largest victory against Mussolini's forces.

A city of 70,000 in 1922, Parma had long enjoyed a radical tradition. Before the First World War it had been the stronghold of revolutionary syndicalists, who gained control of the trades council in early 1907. The two most important activists, Alceste De Ambris and Filippo Corridoni, went on to organise two crucial strikes in 1907 and 1908. In May 1907 agricultural workers surprised the landowners by taking action. Prior to the strike the landowners had refused to negotiate, but after five days of action they signed an agreement giving in to all of the workers' demands.

But the following year the landowners were far better organised. Corridoni later described what happened:

> After 100 days of struggle, which involved 30,000 peasants, the government intervened at the crucial harvest time with the incredible wave of violence everybody has heard about. What with the mass arrest of strike leaders and the general strike called in town to regain physical control of the trades council building, the reorganisation of propaganda and the leadership of the strike took 10 days overall – during which the harvest was chaotically gathered in by several thousand scabs brought in from the surrounding hillsides.[2]

The strike then went down to defeat. Membership of the Parma trades council collapsed – from 28,719 at the start of 1908 to 7,034 at the start of the new year. De Ambris fled to Switzerland, only returning in 1913.[3]

However, compared with other syndicalists and anarchists, De Ambris had a long-term vision of the development of working-class power. Rather than always trying to call and sustain the most radical action without assessing the balance of forces, or suddenly

**77**

unleashing a spontaneous general strike, he weighed each situation up specifically, and on occasion was prepared to retreat. For example, he called off the general strike during the 'Red Week' protests of June 1914 after just two days,[4] despite being fully supportive of what had been a 'political' strike, as opposed to a syndicalist 'economic' strike. Thus he had a wider vision than most syndicalists, and writing in June 1914 he said: 'Yes, I know, it is not a matter of syndicalism in the rigid sense of the word. Syndicalism is carried out on the economic level, and a political struggle is at issue here'.[5] In other words, the left in Parma had a tradition of intelligent tactical manoeuvring and greater openness compared to many other towns. The trades council was situated in the town's most radical district, Oltretorrente, which rich people referred to as 'Zululand' due to its 'wildness'.

However, both De Ambris and Corridoni, in line with most revolutionary syndicalists, supported Italy's entry into the war and then joined up, thus creating a political vacuum on the left in Parma. By the end of the war the syndicalists were divided into the nationalist-oriented 'interventionists', while anarchists were part of the USI union federation.

When people such as Guido Picelli came back to Parma after the war they found workers divided into three competing trades councils – anarchist, socialist and syndicalist. For the rest of his life Picelli argued tirelessly that the left should unite in action against a common enemy.

The political development of Picelli, the undisputed leader of the events of August 1922, is both very important and emblematic in terms of understanding the nature of ADP membership. Born in Parma in 1889, he served as an apprentice watchmaker, then left his family aged 17 to become a travelling amateur actor for six years, joining the Socialist Party at the outbreak of the First World War. As the PSI had a position of neutrality, he volunteered to join the Red Cross, but later could not avoid being conscripted into the infantry.[6] When he returned from the trenches he joined the local Proletarian League, which in Parma contained a healthy mixture of socialists, anarchists and revolutionary syndicalists. He quickly became provincial secretary, as well as also briefly being secretary of the local trades council.[7]

In February 1920 he founded an Autonomous Red Guard to defend local people from fascist attacks. And in autumn 1920 he was one of the main organisers of protests against the sending of locally-based grenadiers to Albania, during which demonstrators placed tree trunks over railway lines – an action for which he was imprisoned.

In April 1921, with Picelli in jail, anti-fascists fought with guns and grenades in a four-hour battle with fascists and police in the Naviglio area of the city, in order to defend their communities and the house of a left-wing MP. Local people came out of their houses to lend support to the anti-fascists. Despite two men being killed, the working class managed to stop the fascist attacks, shouting out from their houses 'Viva the *Arditi del popolo*' and singing *Bandiera Rossa*.[8]

In the general election of May 1921 Picelli was elected as an MP, and under Italian law was therefore released from jail. By now famous in the city, he was carried round the working class areas shoulder high in celebration.[9] Back in the old town of Parma, he 'met with workers, drinking with them round a table, talking and discussing'.[10]

Although Picelli was elected as a Socialist Party MP, he did not join any of the party factions. This basic political understanding, that the moment had come for immediate practical action – rather than the endless arguments that characterised the PSI – was what stood him in good stead. He was neither influenced by the sectarianism of Communists such as Bordiga nor by the nationalist temptations of some of the revolutionary syndicalists.

The other main leader at the Parma barricades was Antonio Cieri, an anarchist. He was born in 1898 and was an *Ardito* in the First World War. He became an activist in his hometown of Ancona, and a draughtsman for the state railways, which then transferred him to Parma in December 1921.

The Parma ADP was founded by Picelli in August 1921, and a few days later 87 members marched through the town.[11] Those with military experience passed their knowledge on to others through regular military training. Finance was obtained by collections in local bars, and by organising local dances and entertainment. Other ADP members built up close relations with soldiers permanently stationed in local barracks, who passed on some weapons and ammunition.[12]

Yet to even begin to call ADP members in Parma war veterans would be inaccurate. The reality of their membership explains to a large degree why anti-fascism became so powerful in Parma. From police files on 31 ADP members, less than half were old enough to have fought in the First World War. The majority of them were builders, porters, industrial workers, small artisans and day labourers.[13]

These early victories had created confidence, but they also encouraged those who were wavering about whether to join the struggle. As Picelli argued on May Day 1922: 'These proud and brave young proletarians knew how to die – but they were not alone. Behind the front line stood an entire community regardless of political allegiances, which made up an invincible army of sympathisers. Young and old, men and women, they've all made a contribution'.[14]

What was inspiring about someone like Picelli was his clear understanding of what needed to be done to defeat fascist squads. Tragically, the national leaders of the left refused to follow the kind of strategy he outlined as early as May 1922:

> When reaction is unleashed and commits massacres, when crimi-nality becomes systematic and is tolerated due to the complicity of the government and judiciary, when the jails are bursting with in-nocent working-class people, when rights are denied to everybody without distinction – Socialists, Communists, trade unionists and anarchists alike – who are under continuous attack and are all equally victims, hit by the very same weapons, then the time has come to stop shouting about your own analysis, or academic discussions, or useless talk about this or that political tactic... The bourgeois united front must be opposed by a working-class one. We will only win if we're united. It is beyond doubt that we are strong, but this strength doesn't make itself felt because it is split up into loads of little groupings who disagree with each other.[15]

Communists in Parma were influenced by this unitary climate. In 1922 the Parma branch numbered 172 members, with 577 members in its youth organisation. The branch had frequently argued with its national leadership over the ADP, and a compromise was eventually reached in which Parma Communists could join the ADP but only if they organised their own separate squads.[16] The unity created in Parma was therefore achieved *despite* the leaderships of the major parties – Communists, Socialists and members of the Catholic-inspired Popular Party went against the official positions of their organisations. And crucially, they were joined by revolutionary syndicalists and anarchists.

Such were the traditions of left-wing activism that in April 1922 30,000 people took part in a march to commemorate the death of a trade union activist 12 months earlier.[17] And the trades council itself took an active part in trying to mobilise workers, as this appeal published on 24 June shows: 'Workers! You have been humiliated, offended, beaten up and threatened. They have offended your family and your women, and beaten up your children. Discover who you are – learn about that wonderful struggle fought 14 years ago. Old people, talk to the youth! Young people, ask your elders!'[18]

It was a city with these traditions that the fascists chose to attack, and the spark came from the general strike called for 31 July. Although it was called off after 24 hours, and was followed by widespread fascist repression throughout the country, Parma decided to carry on. Simultaneously the local ADP, led by Picelli, prepared to resist the inevitable fascist attack.

The fascist leader Italo Balbo, himself an ex-*Ardito* from the war, prepared to head for the city, for reasons he set out in his diary: 'The city has remained almost impregnable to fascism. Due to the weakness of our forces this virtually general strike could not be stopped. Business activities council and government services, and have all ground to a halt over the last three days. The shops are shut. Even the railway station is held by subversives'.[19]

This is why the fascists assembled a huge force from as far afield as Emilia Romagna, Tuscany, the Veneto and the Marches in order to launch their 'punitive expedition' against virtually the only city in Italy which had dared to continue its general strike.

On the other hand, Picelli explained that working-class people had no alternative but to fight, given that 'in towns and cities police chiefs do not take any decision about matters of public order without having first obtained the approval of the local fascist branch… The authorities turn a blind eye to all kinds of fascist violence and provocation. Police chiefs allow fascist branch members to carry a revolver without a licence.' In a very real sense, survival meant working-class people taking the law into their own hands. And if fascism were to win, Picelli continued, it would mean 'suppression of all freedoms and a return to slavery… This is what they mean by loving your country, this is the only real goal fascism is aiming at'.[20]

Balbo and other fascist leaders gave the coming battle central importance in their bid for power:

> The battle about to be fought is far more important than all the others that have preceded it… If Picelli were to win, all the subversives in Italy would raise their heads again. It would show that if red squads arm and organise themselves, any fascist offensive could be neutralised. This example would then be repeated in many Italian cities.[21]

Up to 20,000 well-armed fascists assembled on the night of 1 August. The local police chief promptly told union leaders that he couldn't stop them assembling but, crucially, withdrew his men from the two police stations in the Oltretorrente area, thus giving the fascists a free hand.[22]

However, Picelli and others had called a meeting, and as he later recounted:

> At dawn, when the order was given to get the guns out and launch the insurrection, working-class people took to the streets – as bold as the waters of a river which is bursting its banks. With their shovels, pick-axes, iron bars and all sorts of tools, they helped the *Arditi del popolo* to dig up the cobblestones and tram tracks, to dig trenches, and to erect barricades using carts, benches, timber, iron girders and anything else they could get their hands on. Men, women, old people, young people from all parties and from no party at all were all there, united in a single iron will – resist and fight.[23]

Church towers were used as observation posts, while several priests let church benches be used for barricades, some of which were electrified. Snipers were positioned on roofs and trenches were dug to impede rapid movement, while some strategically important streets and squares were mined. Telegraph poles were knocked down, and telephone wire was stretched across roads to prevent cavalry charges: 'An authentic fortified zone was created, and within that area men, women, the old and the young were under the command of the *Arditi del popolo* and ready for battle'.[24] Shop owners supplied food and drink, as did some priests.

There were about 300 to 400 *Arditi*, divided up into squads of eight to 10 men, armed with pistols, muskets and hand grenades. There were 22 squads in the Oltretorrente area, and six in the Naviglio.[25]

The first fascist attacks came from a group who got off a train and burnt down the railway workers' union office, but the real battle began over control of the bridges leading to the old town. Although they captured one bridge and made limited advances, for four entire days the fascists were repulsed. Picelli's description outlines the tremendous strength of working-class unity:

> Operations also began to improve in the Oltretorrente area – the requisition and distribution of food, first-aid points, field kitchens, patrols, the relaying of information, the reinforcement of defensive positions. Women took a very active part in all of this… Bombs were prepared in houses, along with clubs which included razor blades, knives and nails, as well as acid bombs… Containers full of petrol were distributed to women because, according to our defence plan, if fascists managed to get into Oltretorrente, fighting would then take place on a house by house, alleyway by alleyway, street by street basis. No quarter would be shown – inflammable material would be thrown at the fascists, and our positions would be burned and totally destroyed.[26]

These latter aspects of the defence plan were never in fact put into action. Inside houses, women had prepared various objects to throw out – roof slates, boiling oil, boiling water and small bottles of sulphuric acid.

In any event, the organisation of the defence was democratic first, and military second, as Picelli describes: 'Throughout the fortified zone power passed into the hands of the *Arditi del popolo* command, which was made up of a small number of workers who had been elected previously by the squads'.[27]

Fascist leader Italo Balbo noted many of these activities in his diary: 'Workers operate in shifts. Military discipline… Working-class women bring anti-fascists bread, wine, fruit and potatoes from the kitchen. Rations are distributed twice a day. Meal times are announced by a blast on a bugle. Other blasts indicate lights out and reveille, as well as alarms.' And even worse for him: 'They must have a large quantity of ammunition because they don't spare their bullets, shooting day and night'.[28]

These were the conditions in the Oltretorrente area. However, in the Naviglio area, where anti-fascists were led by the anarchist Antonio Cieri, families were ordered to evacuate, and only a few dozen *Arditi* defended the area. On the second day, anti-fascists in the Naviglio ran the risk of being cut off and surrounded. So the ADP of the Oltretorrente, although severely outnumbered, attacked from their positions singing *Bandiera Rossa*, temporarily relieving the siege. Ammunition was very low in the Naviglio, but supplies were replenished by women acting as couriers.[29]

Fighting raged on day and night for four days, and towards the end ammunition and food were in fact running very low in the old town. Yet the fascists had never broken through.

Then on 5 August the prefect handed over official control of the town to General Lodomez of the army. His officers started to negotiate with local Socialist and trade union leaders, promising them that the fascists would leave once defenders stood down, disarmed and removed their barricades. The general thought he was negotiating with those who were doing the fighting, ie the leaders of the anti-fascist resistance. It was a dangerous moment – these leaders did have some local prestige, but they did not represent the struggle, so potentially their physical and political distance from the fighting risked creating confusion and snatching defeat from the jaws of victory.

Once they heard of the proposal, Picelli and the ADP refused

the general's offer to stand down. What is crucially important
here is not that Picelli was right, but that he had a united and sizeable organisation behind him which agreed with him. And as
the army moved in, recounts Picelli: 'Here they found a different
kind of authority, effectively that of the masses, in the shape of
the *Arditi del popolo*'s command. Nobody had spoken to them but
they couldn't be ignored. Here was their reply: "The trenches
mustn't be touched, as they are a legitimate means of defence
for workers and their communities".' General Lodomez moved his
soldiers into the central areas of the old town anyway, but frater-
nisation took place immediately between soldiers and anti-fascist
workers. Picelli later wrote: 'The mood of the soldiers was such
that it dissuaded the officers from making a big fuss. After two
hours the battalion was withdrawn. Attempts at a compromise
had failed, as did the attempt to disarm the workers'.[30]

The final fascist attack took place in the early afternoon of 6
August, and continued into the night. Once again, the fascists were
repulsed. The following morning the defenders noticed that the
fascists 'were by this stage no longer in military formation, and were
roaming about in all directions in a great rush – with no command
structure – jumping onto trains that were leaving, onto lorries,
bicycles, or on foot'. Balbo phoned Mussolini, who ordered him to
withdraw: 'This wasn't a retreat, but the scattering of large groups
of men who clambered aboard any means of transport they found,
or who ran through the streets, or into the countryside, as if they
were frightened of being chased'.[31] Balbo's own car was shot at as he
left the city.

The fascists suffered 39 dead and 150 wounded, the working
class of Parma five dead and 30 wounded. To give an idea of the
widespread participation, one of the five anti-fascists who died was
Ulisse Corazza, who died with a rifle in his hand fighting alongside
the ADP. Corazza had gone to a Catholic religious school, and
after the First World War was elected as a local councillor for
the Catholic Popular Party.[32]

Spontaneous marches of celebration wound through the city,
red flags were hung from balconies, and when the news reached
the villas of big landowners nearby they quickly disappeared for

several days.[33] As Balbo wrote in his diary, at Parma: 'For the first time fascism found itself facing a well-organised and well-trained adversary – equipped, armed and prepared to fight to the finish'.[34] Of course he forgot to add that the fascists lost the battle!

Yet despite the anti-fascist victory at Parma, nationally Mussolini was just 10 weeks away from becoming prime minister. The defeat his forces had suffered was very much the exception to the rule, but no less significant for that. Years later Mussolini told a biographer, using the euphemism of war veterans for fascists: 'If the Parma model had been used elsewhere, and was successful, the right of war veterans to gain control over public life would have been called into question'.[35]

Picelli immediately sent out trusted activists to various cities to argue the case for replicating the political unity that had led to the military victory in Parma, but their arguments fell on deaf ears. Nevertheless, Picelli continued to spell out the dangers. Writing in a newspaper on 1 October, three weeks before Mussolini took power, he warned:

> The Christian resignation proposed by the masters of the reformist method has made our enemy bold and led to the destruction of our organisations… We have immense strength, but we're disoriented. If we were organised and disciplined we would be strong enough to defeat fascism a thousand times over – this is what we need to understand. We are temporarily in a position of disadvantage because our front is narrow and divided. From a tactical and strategic point of view it is a well-known fact that the narrower your line is, the easier it is for the enemy to concentrate their forces and break through. Therefore our lines must be unified and broadened, to engage our enemy over a wider area.[36]

One worrying sign of the times was that, despite the anti-fascist victory in August, no printer in Parma was prepared to print the newspaper – it was produced in Milan. Yet when the fascists attacked Parma again on 14-16 October the barricades went up again, and they had to retreat.[37]

Years later, while in exile in Paris, Picelli looked back critically on the broader weaknesses of the movement he had led:

Even if the *Arditi del popolo* had managed to pull the mass of working-class people into armed resistance, what was insufficient was the preparatory work among soldiers who, given their mood and specific situation, could have been persuaded to show active solidarity with the proletariat. Similarly insufficient and negative were links with the surrounding provinces, which broke down at the most difficult moments of the struggle. A coordinated peasant movement would have enabled us to immediately launch an offensive.[38]

Despite the August victory in Parma, by now time had run out for Picelli's ideas to make any headway on a national level. There continued to be many acts of heroic resistance, but the prevailing national picture was one of increasing fascist power, which culminated in Mussolini becoming prime minister in October 1922. He was encouraged in this by newspapers such as the *Times*, probably the most influential paper in Europe at the time, which wrote of the fascists in an editorial: 'Their violence may too easily degenerate into excess, but it can only be understood as a reaction against the subversive forces which are undermining the independent existence of the nation'.[39]

The scale of the military problems the left faced also needs to be considered politically, in the sense that the forces of law and order were either tolerating or actively participating in violent fascist attacks. In other words, a political understanding was needed in which anti-fascists clearly realised that to defeat fascism the state also needed to be defeated. But such an understanding, fully developed and centrally placed within a political and military strategy, was by and large lacking within the anti-fascist movement.

Writing in the PSI daily in summer 1921, Socialist leader Pietro Nenni might well have accurately described the problems the ADP faced:

Perhaps the *Arditi del popolo* are deluding themselves when they think they can hold back an armed movement of reaction, when it is under the protection and guidance of the state. As long as the bourgeoisie is in power, it will make use of it against the working class. And the sticks and clubs of the *Arditi del popolo* cannot win against the machine-guns, cannons and aeroplanes of the police state.[40]

But even if this analysis were correct, then one crucial task was to develop the strength of the working class to such a point that not all the 'armed bodies of men' of the state could be relied upon, and at crucial moments would desert or mutiny, or threaten to do so. The logic of Nenni's analysis should have spurred him on to immediately organise working-class self-defence, coupled with a long-term strategy for a revolutionary overthrow of the state. Instead Socialist leaders never called for or organised self-defence, which was urgently needed. If anything, they spent their energies denouncing the bourgeoisie, and when they called for a revolution they only did so in an abstract way.

# The second March on Rome

ADP members continued to resist fascism. It was *Arditi*, among others, who placed barbed wire in front of the king's palace during the March on Rome, in an attempt to dissuade fascists from staging a demonstrative takeover.[41] Yet this second March on Rome was an immense bluff. The military forces fascism had in the field were far from overwhelming. On the morning of 28 October there were only 4,000 men assembled 36 miles to the north west of the capital. There were another 2,000 to the north east, and 8,000 men 15 miles to the east in the town of Tivoli. They were badly armed, with a few machine-guns and just one cannon. All three columns were without food and water, and were not in contact with each other. It was pouring with rain, and most men had neither tents nor a place to stay. But the army garrison alone in Rome contained 12,000 well-equipped and battle-hardened men with tanks and aircraft.[42]

The British ambassador in Rome reported to Marquess Curzon, the British foreign minister, that during the night of 27 October:

Cavalry and armoured cars appeared in the streets, and troops with machine-guns were stationed at the gates of Rome. Light barricades were erected or laid ready for erection across the roads the Fascisti might be expected to advance upon, and barbed wire entanglements were placed at strategical points. Railway lines from the north to Rome were also cut for several hundred yards.[43]

Even if they could organise a coordinated movement towards Rome in the absence of railway lines, the fascists would have been annihilated if they had tried to launch a coup. This was why Mussolini was in Milan, near the Swiss border, and had ordered his offices to be barricaded by barbed wire – hardly a confident leader at the head of his troops.

Yet the military preparations of the Italian state were just sabre-rattling, part of an intricate series of manoeuvres within the ruling class. In reality there was no military plan to stop the fascists. As the British ambassador commented: 'Everybody knew perfectly well that the troops would refuse to take any forcible action whatever against the Fascisti, with whom they were in sympathy'.[44] This was hardly a stunning discovery – collaboration between fascists and the authorities had been growing steadily over the previous two years. In reality, the blackshirts did not try to take power militarily – they were invited to take power by the establishment.

The following morning, 29 October, the king sent a telegram to Mussolini in Milan, asking him to form the next government. The fascist party ended up with five ministries, the Catholic-oriented Popular Party two, Democratic Liberals three, and the conservatives and Nationalists one each.

Just outside Rome that evening one of the three fascist military commanders warned the others not to march: 'Such a move could gravely compromise the outcome of the political negotiations currently in progress, which are heading in the direction of the greatest victory possible'.[45] In reality the first fascist groups moved on the capital the following morning, according to their commander, because 'there were no houses nearby where my soaking men, who had not eaten since the day before, could take shelter'.[46] The British ambassador noticed that most fascists had 'only bludgeons or walking sticks'. Fascists entered Rome in a victory parade rather than as part of a military attack, and their numbers were massively swelled by the knowledge that no fighting would be necessary. Even so, a journalist from the *Times* put the march at no more than 15,000.[47] As part of their celebrations they attempted to penetrate the working-class areas of San Lorenzo, Testaccio and Trionfale but, as in November 1921, were repulsed on every occasion.[48]

Nevertheless, the long dark night of fascism was beginning. Just two days after Mussolini was appointed prime minister the PCI was claiming, in a bluster reminiscent of Mussolini at his most absurd: 'No offensive is possible against such strong and numerous forces.' The reality of the situation was the complete opposite. The very same day Picelli and four other *Arditi* were arrested in Parma.

The tragedy was that all of this could have been avoided. Less than a year earlier large numbers of fascists had been forced to retreat from Rome under police escort, having been outfought by the ADP.

# Why the left failed to fight

There were two main reasons why the left did not seriously mobilise to counter the fascists: (1) the sectarian leadership of the PCI, which refused to build any kind of joint mass movement to fight fascism; and (2) the PSI leadership's belief in parliament, and its traditions of verbal extremism.

It is hard to be sufficiently critical of Amadeo Bordiga in this period. Although he was leader of the PCI from its founding conference in Livorno in January 1921 until his arrest in 1924, his politics have rightly been relegated to the extreme margins of Italian politics ever since. But in those years his dominance of the PCI is beyond question. Bordiga and his 'abstentionist' faction constituted the largest grouping on the 15-man Central Committee elected at Livorno – Bordiga and five others.[1] By comparison, Gramsci had only just managed to get elected to the CC, could not count on any other supporters, and did not even speak at the Livorno conference.

The essential reason for Bordiga's popularity was that he had realised far earlier than Gramsci that the PSI's commitment to a revolutionary strategy was at best hot air. Indeed, he had understood this even before the First World War, and had taken a very hard anti-imperialist line throughout the war. And as Socialist leaders dithered and blustered in the *biennio rosso*, Bordiga's merciless criticism allowed him to build up even more credibility.

The problem with Bordiga was not so much his understanding that a clear break needed to be made from the PSI, but rather the kind of Communist Party he wanted to build.

Unlike Gramsci, Bordiga wanted to build a party of the '*puri e duri*', the 'pure and the hard', which would maintain strict independence from the rest of society. Not only had the PSI held back working-class struggle, so too did the very existence of democracy, Bordiga argued. As the second point in the PCI's founding programme explained: 'The current relations of production are protected by the power of the bourgeois state which, founded on the system of representative democracy, constitutes the defence mechanism for the interests of the capitalist class'.[2]

While Bordiga and his followers were right about the role of the bourgeois state, they were wrong on the issue of democracy. The creation of democracy has by and large been the result of working-class struggle in the face of bitter opposition from the capitalist class. And its very existence, as opposed to non-democracy, makes the working class's ability to organise far greater. This is why Bordiga and his followers were initially not that concerned that fascists were eradicating democracy – after all, the main enemy was capitalism and its bourgeois state.

Therefore one of Bordiga's most fundamental beliefs was that it was always essential to explain to workers that democracy was not enough – that it was a barrier to the creation of socialism. Yet this idea was implemented in quite a literal sense: he had managed to build up a large following within the PSI on the basis of non-participation in elections under any circumstance. Because parliamentary democracy was the main enemy in terms of developing a revolutionary class consciousness, Bordiga consequently had an ambivalent attitude concerning the possibility of a fascist seizure of power. As he wrote in *Ordine Nuovo* on 26 July 1922, with the fascists three months away from taking power:

> So the fascists want to burn down the parliamentary circus? We'd love to see the day! Those collaborationists [Socialist Party leaders] who have always opposed and sabotaged workers' self-defence want a general strike in order to manoeuvre in the current crisis? Great! The main danger is, and remains, that everyone agrees that the apple cart isn't overturned, and that a legal and parliamentary solution is found.[3]

Consequently, the PCI refused all offers of joint work with 'parliamentary' Socialists, as well as with the ADP. As Bordiga had

put it in May 1921: 'Fascists and social democrats are but two aspects of tomorrow's single enemy'.[4] Gramsci too was not immune
to such sectarianism, arguing on 5 July: 'The Socialists will indeed
become the vanguard of anti-proletarian reaction, because they
best know the weaknesses of the working class, and because they
have some personal vendettas to pursue'.[5]

This sectarian stupidity was far more deep-set on Bordiga's
part, as it even continued throughout the early period of Mussolini's dictatorship. Six weeks after Mussolini had taken power
Palmiro Togliatti, who was essentially loyal to Bordiga in this
period, wrote in an article entitled 'The Revolution Defeated?':
'For more than 20 years the Italian working masses have been
conned by electoralist demagogy.' Therefore in some ways the
end of democracy and the victory of fascism were seen as a positive development: 'From a subjective point of view the defeat
of social-democratic opportunism makes it [fascist victory] a revolutionary advancement'.[6]

Another reason for the PCI's hostility to anti-fascist work was
that it misread the nature of the period. Despite the rise in fascist
activity, the recent upsurge of the *biennio rosso* and the revolutionary wave that had recently swept Europe led them to believe
that revolution and not reaction was still the order of the day in
1921-22. Therefore there was very little need for mass anti-fascist
activity. A PCI journal argued in April 1921: 'Even in the camp
of the working class, some people fear and hope that this may be
the beginning of a victorious bourgeois counter-revolution.
However, given the irreversible disintegration of the capitalist
system of production, it can only be the agonised manoeuvres of
a dying organism'.[7] And in the same month Gramsci wrote an
article attacking the reformist Socialist viewpoint: 'The reformists,
in supporting the idea that the current period is one of "reaction",
not only provide a further demonstration of the absolute political blindness caused by parliamentary cretinism, they also show
their willingness to commit high treason against the working
class'.[8]

It must be said that in all of this the PCI leadership did receive some support from the influential president of the Third

International, Grigori Zinoviev. Immediately after Mussolini's seizure of power he rhetorically wondered: 'Is it a coup d'état or a comedy? Perhaps both at the same time. From the historical point of view it is a comedy. In a few months the situation will turn to the advantage of the working class'.[9] In common with many Communist leaders in Italy, Zinoviev refused to acknowledge a profoundly changed situation, and had a tendency to repeat formulas from an earlier but radically different period. Consequently, during a discussion on the situation in Italy at the International's Fourth Congress in December 1922 he stated: 'The objective situation remains revolutionary. Capitalism cannot find sufficient forces within itself to resolve its terminal crisis'.[10]

Within Italy reality was very different to this bluster. Total strike figures were 75 percent to 80 percent lower in 1921 than in 1920.[11] Underlying this was a massive increase in unemployment. From 1 May 1921 to 1 July unemployment rose from 250,000 to 388,000, an increase of 55 percent in just two months, mainly in the industrial North.[12]

As regards what attitude to take towards the ADP, the PCI leadership took a while to make up its mind. After all, the party was only six months old, it was much smaller than the Socialist Party, and it also had to contend with a very large anarchist movement. Some of its suspicion and sectarianism can be understood in this context, although it is a position that is impossible to defend. So after some hesitation the PCI leadership issued an instruction on 7 August that admitted to the reality of what had been happening within the party over recent months: 'Especially in the ranks of Communist youth organisations, many individuals and some party structures have insistently suggested, and even practised, involvement of young and adult Communists in organisations that have arisen outside our party, such as the *Arditi del popolo*.' Their conclusion was unequivocal: 'We can only deplore the fact that Communists have been in contact with the people in Rome who initiated the *Arditi del popolo*, offering to work with them and follow their instructions. If such actions are repeated, the most severe measures will be taken'.[13]

Gramsci took the opposite view. Just a few days later he wrote in support of the *Arditi*, explaining that they were far from being a Socialist Party plot: 'The lightning speed with which the initiative spread was not the result of a general plan prepared by the Socialist Party, but was simply due to the generalised state of mind in the country – the desire to rise up in arms which was smouldering among the broad masses'.[14]

While the PCI committed mistakes on a grand scale, it has to be borne in mind that it was by far the smallest of the two left-wing parties. At its foundation in January 1921 the PCI probably had between 40,000 and 50,000 members, while the PSI had about three times that number. But numbers didn't necessarily mean a more incisive organisation – despite the exit of Communists the PSI remained a highly contradictory and divided party. As one author has noted: 'The contradiction between its Marxist theory and its democratic practice was becoming intolerable, and the party tried to resolve it with the familiar Second International device of "minimum" and "maximum" programmes'.[15] Although the PSI had voted to affiliate to the Communist International at its party congress in Bologna in September 1919, the majority of party members decided not to leave when the Italian Communist Party was formed in January 1921.

No lasting solution that enabled the PSI to act clearly and in a united fashion was ever found. Given such chaos, it is easy to see why Bordiga's faction gained such a following, as it offered 'a total break with *every* bourgeois institution, a rigid Communist Party with a revolutionary programme and action which *nobody* and *nothing* could *blur*'.[16] The dithering and refusal of the PSI leadership to carry forward the struggles of the *biennio rosso* convinced other PSI leaders such as Gramsci – and also the Third International in Moscow – that, initially at least, a clear separation needed to be made between reformist Socialists and revolutionary Communists.

The exit of Communists and the creation of the PCI obviously strengthened the reformist and parliamentary strategy of the PSI leadership around Turati. (The card vote at Livorno was 14,695 for Turati's open reformists, 98,028 for Serrati's centre grouping, and 58,785 for the left – which immediately formed the PCI). Turati's view of fascist violence was that it was the job of parliament and the police to maintain the rule of law. Furthermore, the more PSI leaders talked about 'peace pacts' with fascists in a situation of near civil war, the closer they believed they were moving to government. In some respects Turati and others had an almost 19th-century view of politics and parliament – of a genteel salon of enlightened public-spirited men who came to honourable compromises and agreements. They thought the establishment would always prefer them to the fascists.

The more radical Socialist faction led by Giacinto Serrati had a different but equally disastrous view. They almost welcomed fascist attacks, on the basis that they would force the reawakening of the working class, but until that happened no resistance should be organised. However, probably the main reason for inactivity was their verbal extremism – and consequently a practical refusal to make common cause with any 'progressive bourgeois' elements. There was constant vigilance to ward off any possible 'contamination' from the bourgeoisie.

However, this sterile verbal extremism existed alongside a growing number of fascist attacks. In a private letter written to a friend on 28 April 1921, Serrati quietly admitted to the party's mistake:

> We are living through terrible days. And nothing can be done against such unpunished arrogance because, unfortunately, when everyone was talking about revolution, nobody was preparing it. Now we are the victims of that verbal revolutionary infatuation which deceived a lot of people over the last few months… The bourgeoisie, terrified by our barking, is biting back. And biting hard.[17]

Serrati stayed within the PSI following the creation of the PCI, hoping for some kind of merger with the PCI, which was very quickly encouraged by Moscow. (Serrati subsequently joined the PCI in 1924, although he was to die two years later.)

So, for various reasons, all factions within the PSI were against any self-defence that involved violence. For example, Socialist union leader Giacomo Matteotti (who would be murdered by Mussolini's personal bodyguards three years later) made the following statement in parliament in March 1921, soon after being elected as an MP: 'Stay home! Do not respond to provocations. Even silence, even cowardice, are sometimes heroic'.[18] So even as Mussolini closed down newspapers and arrested hundreds of activists after having become prime minister, Turati continued to believe that appeals to 'the constitution' would preserve democracy and protect the working class from attack.

# The PCI and the question of military resistance

A Communist-oriented journal, *L'Ardito rosso*, was published four times in the autumn of 1920 – several months before the birth of the PCI. Its aim was to organise former soldiers and provide military training for the working class. It also published pamphlets, one of which was called *Form Soldiers' Councils!*[19] Yet the title of this pamphlet also reveals a weakness – the organisation was intended to be more offensive than defensive, another indication of the impending failure of Communist leaders to understand how the situation had rapidly changed after the occupation of the factories.

Once the PCI was created in January 1921 the new party leadership quickly told the leader of *L'Ardito rosso*, Vittorio Ambrosini, to cease all his activities. While he complied with the order, Ambrosini and his supporters joined ADP groups in the summer of 1921.

Many other local leaders of the PCI were also willing to work with the ADP in defence of democracy. Francesco Leone recalls in his home town of Vercelli in summer 1921: 'I called an open meeting for all those who were considering joining the ADP. Our invitation, or appeal, was addressed to all young anti-fascists, but not only to young people. This initiative had a lot of support, including anarchists, who were very numerous in Vercelli at that time'.[20]

The PCI did in fact set up a strictly members-only military organisation. Built around the party's youth organisation, in major industrial areas it had some weaponry salvaged from the end of the occupation of the factories but, by and large, weapons were few and far between. One of the main political tasks of young members was therefore to agitate among conscript soldiers with a view to obtaining arms.[21]

Generally the PCI's overall military strength was quite insignificant. With hindsight, leaders such as Luigi Longo pointed to the absurdity of Bordiga's position: 'We barricaded ourselves behind our Communist squads, which ended up being reduced to a handful of men who were, it must be said, prepared for anything. But they were isolated from the masses, and incapable of building effective barriers against the surging wave of fascist squads'.[22] Interestingly enough, as far as can be established, the majority of ADP activists defined themselves as 'Communists', although most probably weren't members of the PCI.

The following speech made in parliament by PCI MP Nicola Bombacci in May 1922 says all the right things about self-defence. Perhaps even more interesting is that the speech is almost surreal, in that it illustrates how irrelevant parliamentary debates can become in terms of what is actually happening in the streets:

> *Bombacci*: This murder demonstrates once more the need for the working class to arm itself for its own defence. If a general strike had not been called immediately, if the Roman working class had not answered the call of its leaders so enthusiastically, we would not just have suffered the murder which was committed yesterday evening. Dozens and dozens of workers would have been assassinated by premeditated fascist violence! (*loud applause, shouts from fascists*) Workers have no form of defence other than what they create for themselves. While fascists can train, attack, loot, kill and arm themselves with impunity, and while the government is nowhere to be seen – or more frequently supports and encourages fascist violence – how can the working class disarm itself?...
>
> The working class has to arm itself even more!... Recent events give us even greater justification to say to workers: 'If you've got weapons, get them ready. If you haven't got any, find some. Arm yourself for self-defence and for an offensive against the violence of those who exploit you!' (*applause only from Communists*).
> *Giurati* [fascist]: I want this minuted!
> *Bombacci*: Yeah, yeah, let's minute it![23]

But the reality was that the PCI had isolated itself far too much, and in some ways Bombacci was engaging in the sterile bluster typical of the Socialist Party, of which he had been a member until the creation of the PCI. Apart from Gramsci, PCI leaders only started to come to their senses when it was too late.

# The view from Moscow

One of the reasons for the popularity of the PCI was the tremendous prestige of the Bolshevik Party in Russia, which had led a successful revolution in 1917. Subsequently the Bolsheviks took the initiative of setting up the Third International of working-class parties in 1919, also known as the Comintern.

Events had moved very quickly over previous years. When the international revolutionary left held a meeting in the Swiss town of Zimmerwald in 1915, Leon Trotsky joked that they could all be seated in four stagecoaches. Yet just two years later Trotsky was a key leader of a millions-strong working-class revolution in Russia.

The Third International was founded because, in the eyes of the Bolsheviks, the existing Second International had been discredited when nearly all its members – the European Socialist parties – had voted to support 'their' governments in the slaughter of the First World War. Furthermore, the war had ended with mass radicalisation throughout Europe – from Moscow to Glasgow, from Barcelona to Berlin, millions of workers were starting to demand more than what the various Socialist parties were offering, and the Third International wanted to influence them. The invitation to the First Congress of the Comintern, sent out in January 1919, began with the following two points: '(1) The present period is that of the decomposition and collapse of the entire world capitalist system, and will be that of the collapse of European civilisation in general if capitalism, with its insoluble contradictions, is not overthrown. (2) The task of the proletariat now is to seize state power'.[24] Such a statement was not inaccurate – at the time Europe was being swept by a wave of working-class revolutions, although at the same time there was a general lack of experienced revolutionary parties such as the Bolsheviks.

Political clarity was of the essence in such rapidly changing circumstances – something the PSI was clearly lacking – so this is why the Bolsheviks supported Communists leaving the PSI to create a clear revolutionary pole of attraction. They had hoped that Serrati's centrist grouping would leave with the Communists in opposition to the arch-reformist Turati but, in any event, Gramsci later recalled Lenin's advice to Serrati: 'Separate yourselves from Turati, and then make an alliance with him'.[25] A split should not automatically mean increased hostility between new organisations – indeed the formalisation of clear political differences along organisational lines can clear the air, making it easier to work together towards common goals, and thus making it easier for revolutionaries to expose reformist leaders in practice. Through joint action, as the Third International put it in April 1921:

> …the working masses will come to see how the reformists and centrists are daily deceiving them. They will see that the…Turatis and…the MacDonalds do not wish to, and are incapable of fighting either for the dictatorship of the proletariat or even for a crumb of stale bread for the workers. The workers will recognise that the communists are not splitting the proletariat but represent its unifiers in the fight for a better future.[26]

The key problem for the Bolsheviks was that the majority of the Italian working class still gravitated towards the Socialist Party and Serrati. At the end of the Third Congress of the International, Trotsky bluntly reminded the Italian Communist delegates: 'You say that we have stripped them of all their weapons. Perhaps, but they themselves remain. Serrati remains'.[27]

Gramsci later recalled Lenin's original formula of splitting from Turati in order to ally with him in relation to the Communists' own split with the Serrati majority of the PSI: 'This formula should have been adapted by us to the split',[28] or, in other words, the newly born PCI should have made all possible efforts to persuade Serrati to join the new party. Bordiga's leadership simply dogmatically insisted that revolutionary Socialists joined the Communist Party but, as Trotsky argued in July 1921, this was a mechanical stance that avoided the real issue, of 'knowing *how*, and *through what methods* to attract the worker-Socialist into the Communist Party'.[29] Any organisation that thinks it can gain support for revolution by believing that the correctness of its political programme is enough to attract people is doomed to isolation. Again, as Trotsky argued: 'It is necessary by word and deed, by deed and word to conquer the confidence of tens of thousands of worker-Socialists who still remain at the crossroads, but who would like to be in our ranks'.[30]

This was far from being a sterile intellectual debate – there was a real urgency to establishing greater working-class unity and cohesion. After all, Italy went from being on the verge of revolution to fascist dictatorship in just two years. By October 1922, on the eve of Mussolini seizing power, the Third International was now arguing for the merging of the two parties: 'It will of course be no simple matter to amalgamate them, for the task is to amalgamate the proletarian rank and file of these two parties and at the same time to assure a firm revolutionary Communist leadership'.[31] The International was even more explicit in December: 'The general situation in Italy, particularly after the victory of fascist reaction, urgently demands the immediate unification of all revolutionary proletarian forces'.[32] They then set out in detail how the two organisations could merge within two months, thus uniting to fight the common enemy of fascism. But, as Gramsci commented bitterly four years later, Bordiga continued to oppose a merger 'as if it were an implicit disavowal of the Livorno split – a sign of repentance'.[33] However, by now the main problem was not the sectarianism of Amadeo Bordiga – it was the repression of Benito Mussolini.

The unification of political parties can be considered a medium-term or longer-term strategic issue, which ultimately takes on an organisational form. Yet throughout this period Bolshevik leaders such as Lenin and Trotsky were in fact far keener on finding immediate tactical questions that revolutionaries could campaign around in the here and now.

# The united front

By the time of the Second Congress in July-August 1920 many mass working-class parties had joined the Third International or had applied to do so, and other parties were debating the issue. With these mass organisations close to communism, one of the key discussions within the communist movement concerned the dangers of adventurist and sectarian 'ultra-leftism', which would antagonise these organisations new to the communist cause. Indeed, this was the subject of Lenin's booklet *Left-Wing Communism: An Infantile Disorder*, written in preparation for the congress. The final manifesto of the congress, written by Trotsky, put forward a position that was in total contrast to the traditions of Bordiga. Furthermore, it had direct relevance during the occupation of the factories which was to occur in Italy the following month, as well as being applicable to the emerging ADP movement:

> Waging a merciless struggle against reformism in the trade unions and against parliamentary cretinism and careerism, the Communist International at the same time condemns all sectarian summonses to leave the ranks of the multi-millioned trade union organisations or to turn one's back upon parliamentary and municipal institutions. The Communists do not separate themselves from the masses who are being deceived and betrayed by the reformists and the patriots, but engage the latter in an irreconcilable struggle within the mass organisations and institutions established by bourgeois society, in order to overthrow them the more surely and the more quickly.[34]

All of this jarred strongly with the PCI. Bordiga's party, it has to be said, was not the only organisation within the Comintern to put forward a 'theory of the offensive' in which joint work with Socialists was rejected on the basis that they were the working class's worst enemy. Bordiga found he shared some common ground with Zinoviev and leaders of the German Communist Party, the KPD. Put simply, in the words of one of the leaders of the KPD, Ruth Fischer: 'The working class could be moved only when set in motion by a series of offensive acts'.[35] Such a formulation was partly a result of impatience and inexperience, which was the case within the KPD at the time, while for people such as Bordiga the appeal lay in suddenly intervening in working-class politics virtually from the outside.

In any event, the theory was put into practice in Germany in March 1921, when the KPD proclaimed a general strike and then called for an uprising. Leaders of the Comintern such as Zinoviev, Bukharin and Bela Kun had encouraged the inexperienced KPD leadership to launch an insurrection, which quickly went down to defeat. So the 'March Action' was very much 'the child of both the inexperienced German leadership and the Comintern leadership'.[36] Membership of the KPD more than halved, tens of thousands received prison sentences and many activists lost their jobs.

Many of these issues came to a head at the Third Congress of the Comintern, held between 22 June and 12 July 1921 – just three months after the 'March Action' and six months after the creation of the PCI. The view that was now coming to dominate the Comintern was that the working class was suffering from a series of setbacks compared with previous years, and that the most urgent task was gaining majority influence and leadership within it. Trotsky put it thus in his opening speech: 'We can now see and feel that we are no longer close to seizing power in the world revolution. In 1919 we thought it was just a question of months, but now we are saying that it is perhaps a question of years'.[37]

The 'Theses on the International Situation and the Tasks of the Comintern', written by Trotsky, argued: 'The fundamental task of the Communist Party in the current crisis is to lead the present defensive struggles of the proletariat'.[38] As regards the specific realignment of the left in Italy, the 'Theses on Tactics' adopted by the congress welcomed the creation of the PCI but warned that its evolution into a mass force would depend on it 'maintaining close contact with the trade union rank and file during strikes and in the struggle against the counter-revolutionary fascist movement. It also depends on whether the party unites the mass action of the working class and transforms spontaneous action into well-prepared campaigns'.[39]

Despite intense argument over issues such as the 'March Action', in the end the Executive Committee sketched out a method of operation that was in essence the exact opposite of both the reckless adventurism which had been seen in Germany and Bordiga's sectarian isolation. The key task was to win workers away from trade union and Socialist Party bureaucrats, and this could only be done if Communists:

> ...show themselves to be *in the vanguard of the fight by the working class for its everyday needs* and lead the working class in the struggle for an extra slice of bread and for an end to those intolerable burdens which capital increasingly thrusts on the working masses... We will defeat these traitors, these agents of the bourgeoisie, not by theoretical arguments about democracy and dictatorship, *but by taking up the questions of bread and wages, of clothing and housing for the workers*.

> Only by fighting for the basic, day to day needs of the working masses can we create a united proletarian front against the bourgeoisie and overcome the divisions within the proletariat that help maintain the bourgeoisie.[40]

This was the policy of the united front – unity in action from below aimed at a specific goal, whether it be a wage increase, or the defeat of fascists. (This is not to be confused with Stalin's policy of the popular front a decade later. This often involved Communist parties entering into broad national agreements with the leaderships of major bourgeois organisations and political parties.)

The relevance of the united front to Italy, and to many other countries, was the result of a general change in circumstances. The revolutionary tide of 1917-20 had now ebbed, the majority of the working class were no longer closely influenced by revolutionary ideas. Revolutionaries were now in a minority. The united front is an attempt not to engage in broad joint propaganda, but to unite in common action over what are generally rather narrow and specific goals.

What can cause confusion within the united front is a situation in which activists are asked to engage in joint action with organ-isations they had either recently been members of, or had recently been influenced by – such as the Socialist Party. As Trotsky put it in early 1922: 'But, after all, didn't we split with them? Yes, because we disagree with them on fundamental questions of the working-class movement. And yet we seek agreement with them? Yes, in all those cases where the masses that follow them are ready to engage in joint struggle together with the masses that follow us'.[41]

In the Italian case a split had been necessary with the Socialist Party. But that did not mean that any dialogue with Socialists should stop or, crucially, that joint action should stop with PSI members and supporters. A key obstacle here was the 'fortress Communist Party' that Bordiga wanted – a stance that made him unable to see that joint work with others opened up possibilities for revolutionary communism to grow. Apart from being an agreement to take part in joint action, every united front is an arena for political and ideological struggle.

The growing threat of fascism cried out for unity in action on the ground. As Trotsky again stated:

> We broke with the reformists and centrists in order to obtain complete freedom of criticising perfidy, betrayal, indecision and the halfway spirit in the labour movement. For this reason any sort of organisational agreement which restricts our freedom of criticism and agitation is absolutely unacceptable to us. We par-ticipate in a united front but do not for a single moment become dissolved in it. We function in the united front as an independent detachment. It is precisely in the course of struggle that broad masses must learn from experience that we fight better than the others, that we see more clearly than the others, that we are more audacious and resolute.[42]

If the PCI had entered the ADP en masse it would have in all probability provided them with a more stable leadership, and increased their success around the country. A clear united-front approach to Socialists who were already, like many Communists, involved with the ADP as local activists would have increased the likelihood of an ADP united front being able to stop the rising tide of fascist violence, and perhaps have changed the course of Italian history.

# Confusion between Moscow and Rome

To confuse matters further, not only were Bolshevik leaders in dis-agreement with the PCI over the importance of the united front, they were also badly informed. For example Lenin, in a letter to German Communists on 14 August, wrote of a recent ADP demonstration in Rome's Botanical Gardens thus: 'When in July 1921 all the proletariat in Rome – the reformist trade union proletariat and the centrist proletariat of Serrati's party – *followed* the Communists against the fascists, our party achieved *the conquest of the majority* of the working class'.[43] But, as we have seen, although rank and file Communists did take part in this demonstration, the PCI leadership was distinctly hostile to involvement with the ADP.

The Third International's understanding of events in Italy continued to suffer from distortions and inaccuracies over the coming months. For example, on 7 November Ruggiero Grieco, who ran the PCI's organisational bureau, sent a letter to the Comintern's Executive Committee in which he argued:

> Suddenly in July, without any preparation – without anyone in the working-class movement knowing anything beforehand – some military-based groups named the *Arditi del popolo* appeared and declared they wanted to fight fascism. All of this created a very strong reaction. Throughout Italy the proletariat united around this organisation, particularly in those areas where the white gangs had been especially violent. Similar organisations were created, which saw Communists, Socialists, anarchists, Republicans and even Catholics all united, and for a moment it seemed that fascism was going to collapse.[44]

Such a stance – admitting that the ADP had united the left and almost caused the collapse of fascism, while all the time wanting to remain separate from them – was the direct opposite of the united-front policy argued out at the third Comintern congress in the summer. So Grieco justified his party's refusal to be involved with the ADP by making a series of accusations, some of which he probably knew to be untrue:

> The mystery surrounding the birth of the *Arditi* was revealed, and it emerged that they had Nitti to thank for their creation, whose objective was to create an anti-fascist and therefore anti-Giolitti movement. Argo Secondari, the head of the organisation, supported the war, volunteered, became a lieutenant and then a supporter of D'Annunzio. He became notorious last year for being involved in the militaristic 'Pietralata plot' – he was publicly accused of being a police spy and didn't explain himself. All of this gives an idea of the organisation he leads.[45]

The response of the Comintern came in late January 1922, and was probably written by Nikolai Bukharin. In a letter full of sarcasm, he begins by illustrating the PCI's response to the emergence of the ADP:

> Where were the effective leaders of the working masses? Where were the Communists in this period? Were they busy scrutinising the movement with a magnifying glass to see whether it was sufficiently Marxist and in keeping with their programme? We don't believe so. On the contrary – to us it appears that at that moment our young PCI was too weak to be able to dominate this spontaneous movement. The doubt arises that the party's pedantic and formulaic position towards the *Arditi del popolo* was the cause of this weakness... The PCI should have immediately and energetically joined the *Arditi* movement, making common cause with workers and therefore turning petty-bourgeois elements into their sympathisers. Adventurists should have been denounced and removed from positions of leadership, and trusted elements placed at the head of the movement. The Communist Party is the heart and the brain of the working class, and there is no movement in which masses of workers take part which could be too low level and impure for the party.[46]

The sarcasm continued in Bukharin's conclusion: 'For our movement it is always more advantageous to make mistakes alongside the masses rather than far away from them, isolated in a closed circle of party leaders who declare their principled virginity'.[47]

As a leader, Bordiga had led his party into isolation and into prison. Five years later, at the PCI's third congress (held in France due to Mussolini's dictatorship), new leader Antonio Gramsci looked back on his party's failure to ally with the *Arditi* in 1921. He argued that Bordiga's sectarianism 'only leads to passivity and inaction. It consists in the last resort simply in drawing lessons of a purely propagandistic kind from events that have already taken place without the intervention of the party as a whole'.[48]

In essence Bordiga's reaction to his house burning down would be simply to look on, spending all his energy criticising the imperfect skills of the fire crew rather than giving them a hand to put the fire out. Sectarians have very little faith in people's ability to change the world. Much of their energy is spent criticising activists from afar. In essence their self-imposed isolation from the movement means they have very little influence over how struggles develop. Again, as Gramsci put it in 1926, looking back on his party's leadership in 1921-22: '[It] served to disqualify a mass movement which had started from below and which could instead have been exploited by us politically'.[49]

It is obvious that the ADP represented a clear alternative to the inadequacies of both the PCI and the PSI. And it was an alternative that many rank and file Communists and Socialists instinctively wanted to be part of. The tragedy for all concerned was that the Communist and Socialist left never came together around an enlarged ADP to form a united front against fascist attacks.

# Conclusion: then and now

We will never know whether greater unity between the ADP and the left could have stopped fascism.

Yet the activities of the ADP, in embryo, were the only strategy capable of stopping Mussolini. The only significant mistake they made was to prioritise military matters over political issues, and that was essentially a product of the hostility of the rest of the left. But again, the urgency of responding, on their own, to frequent violent attacks by fascists helps to explain why military questions sometimes dominated the organisation's thinking.

If PCI members – often the most politically sophisticated activists – had been involved to a greater extent in the ADP, the organisation would have become more 'political' and would have widened its horizons. The 'united front' policy embodied by the ADP was an absolute necessity in the short term, but it was in essence a defensive response to a strategic decision taken by the ruling class of Italian capitalism. Even if the ADP had managed to defeat fascism, in the long term the working class would still have needed to be mobilised to fight the system – capitalism – which generates fascism.

So the key problem in the development of the ADP was not so much its militaristic attitude but the political mistakes of the established left, which was largely incapable of understanding the mass basis of fascism and the mortal threat it represented. As the main historian of the ADP has written:

> Very few of the 'theorists' of the workers' movement were able to see fascism for what it really was. And among them, only a very small minority attempted to point a way out of the crisis. A theory which does not produce an ensuing praxis is just as unsatisfactory – if not

more so – than a praxis that is not supported by a rigorous analysis.[1]

What has often been forgotten about this period – due to Mussolini's victory – is the weakness and fragility of fascism between 1920 and 1922. Even allowing for the working class's defeat in the *biennio rosso*, there were millions of members in the trade unions, and in the Socialist and Communist parties. The main union federation, the CGL, had 2.2 million members in 1920, while the anarchist-oriented USI federation had 500,000.[2]

But the decline in industrial militancy at the end of the *biennio rosso* did play a role in the victory of fascism. The fascists rarely attacked factories or the heavily industrialised suburbs of cities such as Genoa, Milan and Turin, as they were acutely aware of the power that organised workers still wielded. Instead they concentrated their attacks, and appeals to the working class, in medium-sized towns, which is where the ADP generally developed into unitary organisations. Therefore ADP groups were slow to form in the big cities, and militant anti-fascist work was not developed in these cities, and so the 'big battalions' were not able to be brought into play to help the more beleaguered medium-sized cities and towns.

In any event, the fascist squads did not number more than a few tens of thousands. Renzo De Felice, the most authoritative historian of fascism, has estimated that on 31 December 1919 fascist organisation amounted to just 31 branches and 870 members. The following year membership probably rose to 88 branches with slightly over 20,000 members, and at the end of 1921 there were nearly 1,000 branches and about 250,000 members.[3] In terms of activists prepared to take on the left physically, a major mobilisation held in Naples shortly before the second March on Rome saw 40,000 fascists attending from all over the country. And on the first day that fascists entered Rome the following month there were probably no more than 5,000, rising to a high point over the next couple of days to 25,000.[4] In military terms these are quite small numbers, and the reality was that most of them had come to celebrate – there was very little possibility of fighting, as the existing government and power structure had already agreed that Mussolini would be the next prime minister. In any event, the numbers of fascists mobilised were infinitely lower than the combined forces of the left.

Yet the success of the second March on Rome illustrates that the political system was willing to invite Mussolini into power, even though the military threat was not on a particularly grand scale. But it was the military victories that fascism had scored over the working class that made the Italian ruling class look upon fascists more and more favourably as a force willing and able to thoroughly intimidate the working class. It has been estimated that, in roughly equal numbers, fascist squads and police attacks killed a total of 6,000 working-class people between 1917 and 1922, with tens of thousands being wounded.[5] The political establishment had rewarded widespread political violence and given a small party the central role in the new government – after all, the fascist party only had 35 MPs in a parliament of 535.

Leaders and opinion-makers outside Italy were quick to show their support for Mussolini, with the *Times* commenting the day after he became prime minister: 'Signor Mussolini seems eager to dissipate the apprehensions which have been created abroad by his articles and speeches. There is no doubt that, now he is in power, he will show that he has a full sense of responsibility'.[6] Two days later the British prime minister, Bonar Law, told a public meeting: 'I have received a message from the new head of the Italian government, a friendly message, and I need not say that I have replied on behalf of this country reciprocating that friendly message… Wherever we can practically show our friendship and our sympathy it is our duty to do so'.[7]

Italian fascists in London were immediately given permission to take part in the march past the Cenotaph. And on 16 December, just six weeks after taking power, Mussolini stepped onto the platform at London's Victoria station to be greeted by hundreds of Italian fascists wearing black shirts. The following day he dined with King George V at Buckingham Palace.[8] Indeed the British king was one of the first heads of state to visit Rome, in May 1923. For its part, the *Daily Mail*'s Italian correspondent, Sir Percival Phillips, quickly rushed out a book in praise of fascism – *The Red*

*Dragon and the Black Shirts: How Fascist Italy Found her Soul.*[9]

What emerges from the response of the British ruling class is that anything could be done to the working class to keep it down. Two days after Mussolini took power the British foreign secretary, Lord Curzon, wrote to Mussolini: 'My government entirely shares Your Excellency's confidence in the pursuit of a policy of loyal co-operation between our two countries for the purpose of finding in common a satisfactory solution of the problems confronting them'.[10] Leaving aside the formal diplomatic tone, Curzon was congratulating Mussolini for having defeated one of Europe's most militant working classes – the Italian ruling class had shown that, faced with such a problem, it had no hesitation in turning to the fascists.

Yet British politicians knew exactly what kind of government they were dealing with, and this is best illustrated by events in Turin. The Turinese working class had already resisted two major fascist attacks in April 1921 and July 1922. But in December, two months after Mussolini's seizure of power, another assault was mounted, this time successfully. The British consul in Turin, R L Nosworthy, described what happened:

> The kidnapping and the murders in what might be called the So-cialist quarters of the city…were carried out methodically without the slightest interference from the Royal Constabulary. Not a single arrest has been made. For all practical purposes the Com-munists are regarded as standing outside the protection of the law…and there are still some 20 Socialists and Communists on the proscribed list who are being hunted down for execution.[11]

During three days of attacks at least 11 anti-fascists were mur-dered, and dozens were wounded. One of the victims was Pietro Ferrero, an anarchist and FIOM official, who had led the occu-pation of the factories in 1920. Such was the climate of terror that just five men and 11 women came to his funeral, while FIOM only sent a wreath.[12] Yet two years earlier the Turin working class had been at the centre of a revolutionary opportunity that the left did not take. Now many of these activists were paying the ultimate price for that missed opportunity.

Throughout Europe the ruling class was overjoyed that its class enemy had been decisively beaten in Italy. The analysis made in the following quotation is quite revealing, in that it could have easily have been put forward by somebody like Adolf Hitler. Instead it was made by Winston Churchill, who was speaking to Mussolini in Rome during a press conference held in January 1927:

> Your movement has rendered a service to the whole world. The great fear which has always beset every democratic leader or working-class leader has been that of being undermined or over-bid by someone more extreme than he. It seems that a continued progression to the left, a sort of inevitable landslide into the abyss, was the characteristic of all revolutions. Italy has shown that there is a way of fighting the subversive forces which can rally the mass of the people, properly led, to value and wish to defend the honour and stability of civilised society. She has provided the necessary antidote to the Russian poison. Hereafter, no great nation will be unprovided with an ultimate means of protection against cancerous growths…
>
> If I had been an Italian I should have been wholeheartedly with you from start to finish in your triumphant struggle against the bestial appetites and passions of Leninism.[13]

Many members of the ruling class were often quite at ease at experimenting with some of the same tactics in Britain – in this case, the blurring of any differences between the police and fascists, as the *Times* reported in 1925:

> Liverpool will be the starting point in a new move on the part of the *Fascisti*. Arrangements have been made for members in the Liverpool area to become special constables and to drill at the hall of the City Police. Captain WJ Lewis, commander of the *Fascisti* in the Lancashire and Wirral area, stated that officers of the organisation were to take the oath at police headquarters today, the swearing in of other members in due course… Enquiries indicate that the arrangements will allow the *Fascisti* special constables to be under their own officers.[14]

Apart from Britain, in France the extreme-right organisation *Action française* immediately identified itself fully with the values of fascism and Mussolini's seizure of power.[15] More importantly, across the other side of the Alps a man was writing in his prison cell:

> In this period – I openly admit – I conceived the profoundest admiration for the great man south of the Alps who, full of ardent love for his people, made no pacts with the enemies of Italy, but strove for their annihilation by all ways and means. What will rank Mussolini among the great men of this earth is his determination not to share Italy with the Marxists, but to destroy internationalism and save the fatherland from it.[16]

The importance of such a statement is not that the writer is clearly inspired by Mussolini's rise to power, but the fact that the name of the writer is Adolf Hitler.

But all of this could have been avoided. The battles of Sarzana and Parma, and many others, illustrate that the fascists could have been militarily defeated by determined resistance. The loss of morale and the internal divisions which the fascists suffered were not frequent enough to permanently stem their momentum. Yet overall the tragedy and crucial weakness of the ADP was their political isolation, engineered by the PCI and PSI leaderships, who thus denied the working class an immediately available form of self-defence.

The consequences for Socialists and Communists were disastrous. The PSI collapsed in membership: from a total of 216,327 members at its 17th congress in Livorno in January 1921 to 73,065 at its 19th congress in October 1922, and 10,250 at its 20th congress in April 1923.[17] Over the next 20 years the PSI virtually disappeared from Italy. At some stages the PCI fared little better – in 1926 one leader estimated from exile that it had just 30 active members inside Italy.[18]

As for the ADP, many of their leaders remained politically active. Although many *Arditi* were Socialists, anarchists or even Republicans during 1921-23, if they continued to engage in politics they generally became Communists. Guido Picelli joined the PCI in 1923 and became a PCI MP the following year. He was arrested for the fifth time on May Day 1924, when he flew a red flag from the balcony of parliament. From then until he was given a prison sentence in November 1926 he was repeatedly attacked by fascists. After serving five years he emigrated to France on PCI orders in 1932, from where he was expelled the following year, forcing him to go to Russia and work in a ball bearing factory. He also gave lessons at the Leninist cadre school on military strategy and tactics. In 1936 he volunteered to fight in the Italian Garibaldi Battalion in the Spanish Civil War, arriving in Barcelona in November 1936.[19]

The other main leader at the Parma barricades, Antonio Cieri, continued his anti-fascist activities as an anarchist, both in Italy and France, and, like Picelli, volunteered to fight in the Spanish Civil War in 1936. Due to their military experience both men helped train the first volunteers of the International Brigades. And both men died within a short time of each other: Picelli was shot on patrol in January 1937, while Cieri died three months later at the battle of Huesca. However, former *Ardito* Giuseppe Alberganti survived the Spanish Civil War and went on to become a leader in the anti-fascist Resistance movement of 1943-45 in Italy. After the war he was secretary of the Milan trades council from 1947 to 1958, as well as a PCI MP and senator, and secretary of the city's PCI federation. In 1968 he broke with nearly 50 years of party loyalty and threw in his lot with the far-left student movement until his death in 1980.[20]

But what became of the ADP's leader, Argo Secondari? He was severely beaten up during the second March on Rome, and then placed in Rieti mental asylum in 1924.[21] He remained there for the next 18 years, despite the efforts of his family to take him for treatment to the United States. Apparently he spent most of his days rubbing his hand up and down his thigh, often to the extent of almost rubbing a hole in his trousers. Maybe the failure of the ADP drove him over the edge, but we'll never know.

Perhaps this is a fittingly sad end to a tragic story. It certainly is a shame that, after 18 years in hospital, Secondari died in March 1942 – because had he only lived a year longer he would have seen Mussolini deposed in a palace coup. And two years later he would have seen Mussolini being executed – by a firing squad of armed anti-fascists, part of a new united movement of hundreds of thousands of Communists and Socialists.

But part of what happened in the 1943-45 Resistance movement also explains why the ADP's story has been 'hidden from history'. Ivanoe Bonomi became the first president of the anti-fascist National Liberation Committee in 1943, the first prime minister of Italy in 1944 after the liberation of Rome, and then the first leader of the newly-elected senate in 1946. In all of this he was supported by the Communist and Socialist parties – he was the symbol of anti-fascist unity. How could these two left-wing parties, having supported Bonomi, then bring up his direct role in bringing Mussolini to power and his vicious repression of the ADP when he was minister of the interior?

A disgusting example of modern 'revisionism' has been the recent decision by Italian president Carlo Ciampi to name a new departure lounge at Rome's Ciampino airport after Italo Balbo – the leader of the attack on Parma in August 1922, and of many other mass attacks during the fascists' rise to power.[22]

# Lessons for today

But all of this is not just ancient history. The threat of fascism has not disappeared, particularly in Italy. Anybody who attended the great anti-capitalist demonstration in July 2001 against the G8 summit in Genoa would have a good inkling of what happens when fascist ideas gain influence within the police.

Of all the various security forces unleashed on demonstrators, it was probably the *carabinieri*, the militarised police force, that committed the worst excesses. They had been officially designated 'the fourth armed force' – after the army, navy and air force – not by Silvio Berlusconi's right-wing government, but by the centre-left government that had been in power until just two months before the Genoa demonstrations. This occurred despite the fact that the authorities were well aware of the anti-democratic views within the organisation.[23]

On Saturday 21 July deputy prime minister Gianfranco Fini, leader of the 'post-fascist' National Alliance, spent four hours on a visit to the *carabinieri*'s centre of operations. Another National Alliance MP, an ex-*carabiniere* himself, also paid a visit. And it was a *carabiniere* who murdered Carlo Giuliani in Genoa. Some politicians from *Forza Italia*, Silvio Berlusconi's party, immediately announced they wanted to offer him a free holiday in the hotels they owned in southern Italy.

The only surprising thing about police violence in Genoa was that other protesters weren't killed by bullets, as 18 live rounds were fired during the demonstrations. It was equally surprising that no demonstrators died from the various items of weaponry used in police attacks, including the 6,000 teargas canisters fired, often directly into the crowd.

And the violence didn't stop once the demonstrations were over – special forces then raided protesters sleeping at a local school, taking them off to a police barracks for 'questioning'. When those arrested arrived at Bolzaneto barracks they were forced to shout '*Viva il duce!*', and police constantly played fascist songs on their mobile phones. One policeman stationed there later admitted: 'You could see a few swastikas around.' Another recounted in greater detail:

> As people got out of the vans they were hit. They made them stand up against the wall. Once they got inside they banged their heads against the wall. They pissed on some of them. And they beat others up if they didn't sing *Faccetta Nera* [a fascist song]. One girl was vomiting blood and they just stood by watching her. They threatened to rape some girls with their truncheons.
>
> Our commanding officer is a hard man, but he's old-fashioned as well. He has a sense of morals and he knows how to educate his men. We call him Rommel.

A freelance photographer taken to the same barracks recalls that:

> …the soundtrack of this horror movie was a repetitive chant which the riot police know by heart. And unfortunately, I too can now remember every word:

*One two three, viva Pinochet*
*Four five six, kill all the dirty Yids*
*Seven eight nine, hang wogs out on the line.*[24]

One demonstrator, a steel worker whose colleagues went on strike to demand his release, was arrested when wearing a T-shirt which showed his left-wing sympathies. In the barracks the police, when they weren't hitting him, were reminding him of Silvio Berlusconi's new government and what they thought it meant for them: 'With this new government the good times have ended for all you Communists. You'd better learn to stay home, otherwise we'll kill the lot of you'.[25]

These blatant fascist sympathies were revealed again during the public outrage following police violence in Genoa. A few weeks afterwards a right-wing police association distributed a leaflet within the Rome police headquarters entitled 'Thank You, Heroes', addressed to those officers who had been on duty in Genoa. Part of it read: 'It is thanks to you that for a few days we all felt united again, something that hasn't happened for many years'.[26]

Despite these problems, the anti-capitalist movement has shown great strength. The big demonstrations in Genoa and Barcelona have brought people together, and taught them the importance of having hundreds of thousands of people on the streets – of safety in numbers.

A political common sense has arisen in which many political forces have understood that it is essential to be inside the anti-capitalist movement, trying to influence its general direction and winning groups of people to your own position. Any groups which stay outside not only condemn themselves to irrelevance, they also fail to contribute to the growth of a mass movement.

Yet, just as in Italy in 1921-22, there are those who condemn the anti-capitalist movement for its lack of clarity and its growing reformism, while choosing not to influence it in any way. Others, also outside the movement, still hope against hope that the system can reform itself, and the injustices and violence of capitalism can be miraculously solved.

But the threat of fascism extends way beyond Italy, and so often there are parallels with Mussolini's rise to power.[27] Although there is not yet a crisis as deep as the 1920s and 1930s, there is nevertheless a growing bitterness against mainstream politicians.

So for example in France, the fascist National Front gained 5.5 million votes in the final round of the 2002 presidential elections. The underlying reason for this was that in recent years establishment politicians, of both the left and right, made the National Front's policies respectable by either implementing some of them or by doing electoral deals with them.[28] In Holland the racist Pim Fortuyn List is the second largest party in the Dutch parliament, and currently holds four ministries, including the newly created Ministry for Immigration and Integration.

And in Britain three British National Party councillors were elected in Burnley in May 2002. The response of Tony Blair was to announce a series of restrictions on the rights of asylum seekers, further legitimising racism and the far right. This sometimes goes as far as proposing openly far-right policies, such as Blair's idea to send gunboats to patrol the Mediterranean to protect the shores of 'Fortress Europe' from asylum seekers. Gianfranco Fini, Italian deputy prime minister and a direct political descendant of Benito Mussolini, greeted the proposal warmly: 'This is a serious policy in terms of limiting immigration.' He then went on, using Blair's policy to attack the Italian left: 'He's the one who has got serious policies to control immigration. The Italian left is still stuck inside ideological cages'.[29]

Yet it is in Britain that a campaigning organisation with some similarities to the ADP exists – the Anti Nazi League. Involving Christians, Muslims, trade unionists, revolutionary socialists, Labour Party members and pensioners, it has two simple strands to its activities: (1) the exposure of people pretending to be democrats as Nazi Hitler-lovers; and (2) militant campaigning to ensure that the Nazis never gain a stable foothold in society.

The ANL, like the ADP in the early 1920s, does not shy away from physically confronting Nazis, whether it be through wiping out fascist slogans or flyposting, or countering their attempts at mass leafleting, marching or holding public meetings. Not only does this demoralise them and discourage wavering members of far-right organisations from taking part, it often brings the violent Nazi nature of the hardcore to the surface, thus undercutting their support even further.

The ANL is a united front aimed at bringing together the many people outraged and disgusted by the activities of organised fascists. But these anti-fascist organisations exist to combat the symptoms of a disease, not its cause. It is capitalism that repeatedly creates war, recession, unemployment and bad housing in the first place, allowing Nazis to exploit people's anger over these conditions by scapegoating minorities.

And it is over how to deal with capitalism that a broad anti-fascist movement can find itself disagreeing over what solutions should be offered. There are those who argue that things should go no further than gaining reforms within a parliamentary system, and that the police must uphold the rule of law. The experience of Italy in the early 1920s – including the enthusiasm of the British ruling class for Mussolini's regime – Germany in the early 1930s, and many other examples, show that the problem of fascism is deeply embedded within capitalism.

Stopping the fascist threat requires revolutionary socialist politics – this was as true in 1922 as it is in 2002. In the first instance this means a united fight against an immediate fascist threat, as well as encouraging working-class people to defend their jobs and public services. But, in the long term, eradicating the threat of the far right means overthrowing a system which in times of crisis will have no qualms in turning to the blackshirts to defend its power and privileges. In short, a revolutionary party is needed to educate and organise together with workers in order to move towards that 'other world' which is not only possible, but absolutely necessary in a capitalist system that permanently harbours the germs of fascist barbarism.

# Notes

## Introduction

1   G Picelli, 'La rivolta di Parma', *Lo Stato Operaio*, no 10 (1934), pp754-755, 758.

2   *Del popolo* literally means 'of the people', while *Arditi* were shock troops in the First World War. So the three Italian words could roughly be translated as 'the people's shock troops'.

3   I Fuschini, *Gli arditi del popolo* (Ravenna: Longo Editore, 1994), p25.

## A place called Italy

1   D Horowitz, *The Italian Labor Movement* (Cambridge, Mass: Harvard University Press, 1963), p21.

2   Quoted in A Davidson, *The Theory and Practice of Italian Communism* (London: Merlin Press, 1982), p17.

3   Quoted in N Pernicone, *Italian Anarchism 1864-1892* (Princeton: Princeton University Press, 1993), p84.

4   Quoted in C Pillon, *I comunisti nella storia d'Italia*, vol 1 (Il calendario del popolo: no place or date of publication), p22.

5   D Horowitz, op cit, p35.

6   Ibid, p41.

7   L Tilly, *Politics and Class in Milan 1881-1901* (Oxford: Oxford University Press, 1992), p222.

8   T Behan, *The Long Awaited Moment: The Working Class and the Italian Communist Party in Milan 1943-1948* (New York: Peter Lang, 1997), p26.

9   Many historians estimate these to be only about half of the real number of casualties. See M Clark, *A History of Modern Italy 1870-1983* (London: Longmans, 1986), p104. A month later the king gave the commanding officer, General Bava Beccaris, an award for bravery.

10   D Horowitz, op cit, p36.

11   Quoted in A Davidson, op cit, pp27-28.

12   Ibid, p30.

13   Quoted ibid.

14   Quoted in L Cortesi, *Le origini del PCI* vol 1 (Bari-Rome: Laterza, 1977), p3.

15   Quoted ibid, p65.

16   Ibid, p68.

17   L Tilly, op cit, p277.

18   D D Roberts, *The Syndicalist Tradition and Italian Fascism* (Manchester: Manchester University Press, 1979), p57.

19   T Cliff and D Gluckstein, *The Labour Party: A Marxist History* (London: Bookmarks, 1988), pp52-53. Emphasis in original. It would be wrong to make a straight comparison between the British labour movement and Labour Party and their Italian equivalents. The Italian working class tended to be generally more militant than their British counterparts, and consequently trade union federations were far more independent of the PSI.

20   R Del Carria, *Proletari senza rivoluzione*, vol 1 (Milan: Edizioni Oriente, 1970), pp377-387.

21   G Williams, *Proletarian Order: Antonio Gramsci, Factory Councils and the Origins of Communism in Italy 1911-1921* (London: Pluto Press, 1974), p27.

22   R Del Carria, op cit, p363.

23   D Horowitz, op cit, p176.

24   G Williams, op cit, p51.

25   Quoted in P Alatri, 'L'interventismo e la guerra', in Aa.vv (eds), *Storia della società italiana: La disgregazione dello stato liberale* (Milan: Teti editore, 1982), p15. Obviously the revolutionary wave at the end of the First World War was to prove Pareto wrong.

26   Quoted in D Guerin, *Fascism and Big Business* (New York, Monad, 1973), p173.

27   G Williams, op cit, p50.

28   P Alatri, op cit, p26.

29   Quoted ibid, p29.

30   M Rossi, *Arditi, non gendarmi! Dall'arditismo di guerra agli Arditi del popolo* (Pisa: Biblioteca Franco Serantini, 1997), p17.

31   M Blinkhorn, *Mussolini and Fascist Italy* (London: Routledge, 1994), p13.

32   J Ridley, *Mussolini* (London: Constable, 1997), p84.

33   D Horowitz, op cit, p130.

34   I Fuschini, op cit, p10. The groups were also called *Arditi d'Italia*.

35   M Rossi, op cit, pp13-14.

36   I Fuschini, op cit, p11.

37   M Rossi, op cit, p18.

38   Ibid, pp15-16.

39   Ibid, p22.

40   E Francescangeli, *Arditi del popolo: Argo Secondari e la prima organizzazione antifascista* (Rome: Odradek, 2000), p15. Emphasis in original.

41   G Procacci, *Dalla rassegnazione alla rivolta: Mentalità e comportamenti popolari nella grande guerra* (Rome: Bulzoni, 1999), p197. The 2,086,046 strike days of 1914 were in large part due to the 'Red Week' of semi-insurrections which took place in June.

42   P Corner, *Fascism in Ferrara 1919-1925* (Oxford: Oxford University Press, 1975), pp49-50.

# The Italian left

1 P Alatri, op cit, p17.
2 G Bocca, *Palmiro Togliatti* (Rome: L'Unità, 1992), p41.
3 D Horowitz, op cit, p141.
4 Ibid, p177.
5 M Rossi, op cit, p25.
6 Quoted in D Horowitz, op cit, p134.
7 Quoted in I Barbadoro, 'Biennio rosso', in Aa.vv (eds), *Storia della società italiana*, op cit, p270.
8 D Horowitz, op cit, pp133-134.
9 Quoted in I Barbadoro, op cit, p248.
10 Ibid, pp253-254.
11 G Bocca, op cit, p45.
12 Quoted in I Barbadoro, op cit, p258; D Horowitz, op cit, p139.
13 N S Onofri, '1913-1922, un decennio storico per Bologna: dalla rivoluzione rossa alla reazione nera', in L Casali (ed), *Bologna 1920: Le origini del fascismo* (Bologna: Cappelli, 1982), p71.
14 I Barbadoro, op cit, p260.
15 Quoted ibid, p261.
16 Quoted ibid, p267.
17 Quoted ibid, p273.
18 G Williams, op cit, p193.
19 I Barbadoro, op cit, p275.
20 M Rossi, op cit, p59.
21 E Francescangeli, op cit, p40.
22 Quoted in D Hallas, *The Comintern* (London: Bookmarks, 1985), p58.
23 D Horowitz, op cit, p141.
24 Ibid, p142.
25 I Barbadoro, op cit, p268.
26 Quoted ibid, p278.
27 Quoted in J Ridley, op cit, p102.
28 *Il Corriere della Sera*, 31 August 1920, quoted in P Spriano, *The Occupation of the Factories* (London: Pluto Press, 1975), p54.
29 B Guidetti Serra, *Compagne. Testimonianze di partecipazione politica femminile*, vol 1 (Turin: Einaudi, 1977), p130. Red Guards existed in several factories, prepared for attacks either by fascists or police. In reality they had very little weaponry. Generally they used guns left by security guards or soldiers stationed within the factory, or alternatively rudimentary weapons built by workers.
30 D Horowitz, op cit, p149.
31 G Maione, *Il biennio rosso: Autonomia e spontaneità operaia nel 1919-1920* (Bologna: Il Mulino, 1975), p243.
32 P Spriano, op cit, p181.
33 G Bocca, op cit, p55.
34 P Spriano, op cit, p56.

35   G Maione, op cit, p251.
36   Quoted ibid, p250.
37   M Clark, *Antonio Gramsci and the Revolution that Failed* (New Haven: Yale University Press, 1977), p72.
38   See G Williams, op cit, pp197-198.
39   After the occupation of the factories, Ferrero moved closer to Gramsci and the Communists, sometimes writing in *Ordine Nuovo*. See C Levy, *Gramsci and the Anarchists* (Oxford: Berg, 1999), p224.
40   Quoted in D Horowitz, op cit, p150.
41   Quoted in I Barbadoro, op cit, p284.
42   Quoted in G Sacchetti, C Ferrari and M C Cabassi, *Ricordo di uomini e lotte del 900* (Florence: Ancora in marcia!, 2000), p87.
43   Quoted in D Guerin, op cit, p49.
44   L Trotsky, *The First Five Years of the Communist International*, vol 1 (London: New Park, 1973), p314.
45   Quoted in P Corner, op cit, p101.

# The rise of fascism

1    E Francescangeli, op cit, pp26-27.
2    F Carsten, *The Rise of Fascism* (London: Methuen, 1970), p50.
3    E Francescangeli, op cit, p24.
4    Viscount Templewood (Samuel Hoare), *Nine Troubled Years* (London: Collins, 1954), p154.
5    Quoted in J Ridley, op cit, p94.
6    E Francescangeli, op cit, p41.
7    Mussolini was writing on 26 February 1920. Quoted in D Horowitz, op cit, p155.
8    M Rossi, op cit, p37.
9    E Francescangeli, op cit, pp18-19.
10   R De Felice, *Mussolini il fascista: La conquista del potere* (Turin: Einaudi, 1966), pp766-767.
11   L Cortesi, op cit, vol 2, p272.
12   I Fuschini, op cit, p85.
13   Quoted in M Clark, 'Italian Squadrismo and Contemporary Vigilantism', *European History Quarterly*, vol 18 (1988), p39.
14   P Corner, op cit, pp146-147.
15   A Gramsci, *Socialismo e fascismo: L'Ordine Nuovo 1921-1922* (Turin: Einaudi, 1966), p200.
16   R De Felice, op cit, p8.
17   D Horowitz, op cit, p165. The PSI's number of MPs decreased from 156 to 123, while the PCI had 15 MPs. The fascists gained 35 seats.
18   M Clark, *Antonio Gramsci and the Revolution that Failed*, op cit, p207.
19   G Williams, op cit, p292.

20  E Francescangeli, op cit, pp43-44.
21  Ibid, p43.
22  N Revelli, *Il mondo dei vinti* (Turin: Einaudi, 1979), p251.
23  C Bermani, '"Forze dell'ordine" e continuità dello Stato', in Aa.vv (eds), *Guerra civile globale* (Rome: Odradek, 2001), p139. In September 1922 five anarchists were on the verge of killing the king, only to be discovered by the police at the last minute. See L Di Lembo, *Guerra di classe e lotta umana: L'anarchismo in Italia dal biennio rosso alla guerra di Spagna* (Pisa: Biblioteca Franco Serantini, 2001), p141.
24  L Trotsky, *Against Individual Terrorism* (New York: Pathfinder, 1974), p7.
25  Quoted in D Horowitz, op cit, p156. The 'Black and Tans', so named because of the colour of their uniforms, were an extremely brutal auxiliary force of the British army, sent to Ireland in 1920-21 to stop the fight for independence. In a relatively short period they murdered many Republicans, their sympathisers, or individuals not even involved in political struggle. They also destroyed 800 houses and 900 shops, as well as burning down Cork city centre.
26  E Lussu, *Marcia su Roma e dintorni* (Milan: Mondadori, 1968), p23.
27  P Corner, op cit, p ix.
28  M Rossi, op cit, p107.
29  C Bermani, op cit, p117.
30  Ibid, p118.
31  I Balbo, *Diario 1922* (Milan: Mondadori, 1932), p63.
32  Quoted in L Di Lembo, op cit, p135.
33  See A Tasca, *Nascita e avvento del fascismo* (Florence: La Nuova Italia, 1995), pp344-360.
34  Public Record Office: FO 371/7658.
35  P Spriano, *Storia del partito comunista: da Bordiga a Gramsci* (Turin: Einaudi, 1967), p211.
36  M Rossi, op cit, p127.
37  A Tasca, op cit, p355. Incredibly, this is about £7 million at today's prices.
38  Public Record Office: FO 371/7659. Memo dated 7 August 1922.
39  E Francescangeli, op cit, p130.
40  Public Record Office: FO 371/7659. Memo dated 7 August 1922.
41  Ibid. Memo dated 8 August 1922.
42  *Times*, 2 August 1922.
43  M Rossi, op cit, p144.
44  D Horowitz, op cit, p171.
45  *Ordine Nuovo*, 23 August 1922.

# Who were the *Arditi del popolo*?

1  For an early manifesto see M Rossi, op cit, pp167-169.
2  E Francescangeli, op cit, pp18-19.
3  Quoted in M Rossi, op cit, p28.

4   Ibid, p29.
5   Ibid, p31.
6   I Fuschini, op cit, p38.
7   T Abse, *Sovversivi e fascisti a Livorno* (Milan: Franco Angeli, 1991), pp171-172.
8   M Rossi, op cit, p88.
9   E Francescangeli, op cit, p51. On Turin see A Sonnessa, *The Resistance of the Turin Working Class to the Rise of Fascism: Political and Community Responses 1921-1925* (PhD, Goldsmiths' College, University of London, 2002).
10  Quoted in L Di Lembo, op cit, p125.
11  M Rossi, op cit, p106.
12  E Francescangeli, op cit, p52.
13  M Rossi, op cit, p73.
14  Ibid, p80.
15  Ibid, pp81-86.
16  Ibid, p89.
17  E Francescangeli, op cit, p54. The second and third manifestos, published in July, were much more left wing.
18  Ibid, p57. The equivalent is about £7,000 today.
19  I Fuschini, op cit, p43.
20  *Ordine Nuovo*, 6 July 1921.
21  Quoted in I Fuschini, op cit, p46.
22  *Ordine Nuovo*, 7 July 1921.
23  Central State Archives (ACS): M I Div affari generali e riservati, 1922, b98, f44. Memo dated 8 July 1921.
24  E Francescangeli, op cit, p57.
25  Ibid, p67.
26  M Rossi, op cit, p91.
27  E Francescangeli, op cit, p62.
28  See I Fuschini, op cit, p93.
29  Ibid, p94.
30  Reproduced in M Rossi, op cit, pp175-176.
31  Ibid, p95.
32  E Francescangeli, op cit, p64.
33  Ibid, p261.
34  *Ordine Nuovo*, 28 July 1921.
35  E Francescangeli, op cit, p68.
36  A Gramsci, *Selections from Political Writings (1921-1926)* (London: Lawrence and Wishart, 1978), p57.
37  Ibid.
38  E Francescangeli, op cit, p65.

# Stopping fascism

1    I Fuschini, op cit, pp57-58.
2    E Francescangeli, op cit, p260. Indeed, one of the key factors that caused the fascist defeat was, unusually, police resistance to fascist aggression.
3    *Il Manifesto*, 19 July 2002.
4    I Fuschini, op cit, p58. The *fascio* was the equivalent of a local party branch.
5    A Tasca, op cit, p264.
6    *Il Manifesto*, 19 July 2002.
7    See I Fuschini, op cit, pp59-60; E Francescangeli, op cit, p260.
8    Quoted in A Tasca, op cit, p264.
9    R De Felice, op cit, p139.
10   Quoted in E Francescangeli, op cit, p97.
11   Quoted in I Fuschini, op cit, p82.
12   R De Felice, op cit, p143.
13   Quoted ibid, p144.
14   Quoted ibid, p149.
15   Quoted in E Francescangeli, op cit, p82.
16   Quoted in R De Felice, op cit, p150.
17   Quoted ibid, p151.
18   Quoted in A Gramsci, *Selections from Political Writings (1921-1926)*, op cit, p60.
19   E Francescangeli, op cit, p99.
20   Quoted ibid, p100.
21   G Alberganti, *Autobiografia di un sovversivo, 1898-1923* (Milan: Quaderni dell'Archivio della CGIL di Milano, 1996), p70.
22   Quoted in E Francescangeli, op cit, p101.
23   G Alberganti, op cit, p71.
24   E Francescangeli, op cit, pp56-57.
25   Quoted ibid, p102.
26   I Fuschini, op cit, pp89, 95.
27   E Francescangeli, op cit, p110.
28   M Rossi, op cit, p107.
29   Ibid, p105.
30   I Fuschini, op cit, p86.
31   *Ordine Nuovo*, 15 November 1921.
32   Ibid, 10 November 1921.
33   M Rossi, op cit, p114.
34   R Del Carria, op cit, p200.
35   E Francescangeli, op cit, p264.
36   *Ordine Nuovo*, 11 November 1921.
37   Ibid, 12 November 1921.
38   Ibid.
39   E Francescangeli, op cit, p264; M Rossi, op cit, p116.
40   *Ordine Nuovo*, 13 November 1921.

41   Ibid, 14 November 1921.
42   R De Felice, op cit, p184.
43   R Del Carria, op cit, p201.
44   E Francescangeli, op cit, p122.
45   *Ordine Nuovo*, 14 November 1921.

# *Parma bell'arma*

1   The words *bell'arma* mean 'beautiful weapon', and rhyme with the name of the city.
2   Quoted in M Minardi (ed), *Pro Memoria: La città, le barricate, il monumento* (Parma: Comune di Parma, 1997), p44.
3   D D Roberts, op cit, p86.
4   Ibid, p74.
5   Quoted ibid, p102.
6   E Francescangeli, op cit, p132.
7   M Rossi, op cit, p128.
8   R Del Carria, op cit, p207.
9   D Gagliani, 'Guido Picelli', in Aa.vv (eds), *Dietro le barricate: Parma 1922* (Parma: Comune di Parma, 1983), p174.
10  R Del Carria, op cit, p207.
11  D Gagliani, op cit, p176.
12  G Picelli, op cit, p754.
13  M Rossi, op cit, p130.
14  Quoted in M Minardi, op cit, p42.
15  R Del Carria, op cit, p191; M Rossi, op cit, p129.
16  M Rossi, pp131-132.
17  Ibid, p132.
18  Quoted in M Minardi, op cit, p46.
19  I Balbo, op cit, p115.
20  Quoted in M Minardi, op cit, p52.
21  I Balbo, op cit, p118.
22  G Picelli, op cit, p754.
23  Ibid, p755.
24  I Fuschini, op cit, p69.
25  G Picelli, op cit, p755.
26  Ibid, pp756-757.
27  Ibid, p755.
28  I Balbo, op cit, p117.
29  G Picelli, op cit, p756.
30  Ibid, p757.
31  Ibid, p758.
32  M Minardi, op cit, pp19-20.
33  G Picelli, op cit, p758.

34   I Balbo, op cit, p119.
35   Quoted in M Minardi, op cit, p37.
36   Quoted in E Francescangeli, op cit, p142.
37   D Gagliani, op cit, p177.
38   G Picelli, op cit, p760.
39   *Times*, 12 August 1922.
40   Quoted in M Rossi, op cit, p159.
41   I Fuschini, op cit, p23.
42   A Tasca, op cit, p467.
43   Public Record Office: FO, 371/7659. Memo dated 31 October 1922.
44   Ibid.
45   A Tasca, op cit, p468.
46   Ibid, p469.
47   *Times*, 1 November 1922.
48   E Francescangeli, op cit, p141.

# Why the left failed to fight

1   P Spriano, *Storia del partito comunista italiano*, op cit, p117.
2   Quoted in L Cortesi, op cit, vol 2, p303.
3   Quoted in P Spriano, *Storia del partito comunista italiano*, op cit, p205.
4   Quoted in E Francescangeli, op cit, p90.
5   A Gramsci, *Selections from Political Writings (1921-1926)*, op cit, p54. However, Gramsci's view began to change significantly the very same month, probably as a result of the creation of the ADP and their rally in Rome. See the next article in this volume, 'The *Arditi del popolo*', pp56-58. The tragedy though was that he was not yet in a dominant position within the party.
6   Quoted in G Bocca, op cit, p83. The article is dated 9 December 1922.
7   Quoted in E Francescangeli, op cit, p90.
8   Ibid. Gramsci's article was published on 23 April.
9   Quoted in A Rosmer, *Lenin's Moscow* (London: Bookmarks, 1987), p207.
10  Quoted in A De Clementi, *Amadeo Bordiga* (Turin: Einaudi, 1971), p171.
11  N Poulantzas, *Fascism and Dictatorship* (London: New Left Books, 1974), p199.
12  *Ordine Nuovo*, 7 July 1921.
13  Quoted in M Rossi, op cit, p140.
14  A Gramsci, *Selections from Political Writings (1921-1926)*, op cit, p62. Gramsci was writing on 19 August.
15  G Williams, op cit, p25.
16  Ibid, p34. Emphasis in original.
17  Quoted in P Spriano, *Storia del partito comunista italiano*, op cit, p123.
18  Quoted in D Guerin, op cit, p109.
19  E Francescangeli, op cit, p93.
20  Quoted in P Spriano, *Storia del partito comunista italiano*, op cit, p143.
21  Ibid, p171.

22   Quoted in I Fuschini, op cit, p79.
23   Quoted in *Ordine Nuovo*, 28 May 1922.
24   Quoted in A Adler (ed), *Theses, Resolutions and Manifestos of the First Four Congresses of the Third International* (London: Ink Links, 1980), p1.
25   A Gramsci, *Selections from Political Writings (1921-1926)*, op cit, p380.
26   L Trotsky, *The First Five Years of the Communist International*, op cit, vol 1, p202.
27   Ibid, p369.
28   A Gramsci, *Selections from Political Writings (1921-1926)*, op cit, p380.
29   L Trotsky, *The First Five Years of the Communist International*, op cit, vol 2, p15. Emphasis in original.
30   Ibid, p16.
31   Ibid, p211.
32   A Adler, op cit, p371.
33   A Gramsci, *Selections from Political Writings (1921-1926)*, op cit, p380.
34   A Adler, op cit, pp168-169.
35   Quoted in D Hallas, op cit, p62.
36   T Cliff, *The Bolsheviks and World Communism* (London: Pluto Press, 1978), p72.
37   P Spriano, *Storia del partito comunista italiano*, op cit, p156.
38   A Adler, op cit, p202.
39   Ibid, pp280-281.
40   Ibid, p302. Emphasis in original.
41   L Trotsky, *The First Five Years of the Communist International*, op cit, vol 2, p95.
42   Ibid, p96.
43   Quoted in E Francescangeli, op cit, p103. Emphasis in original.
44   Ibid, pp104-105.
45   Ibid. Nitti and Giolitti were establishment politicians, vying to be prime minister. Giolitti resigned as prime minister on 27 June; about the same time as the emergence of the ADP. See the chapter "Who were the *Arditi del Popolo*?' for details of the 'Pietralata plot'.
46   Ibid, p106.
47   Ibid, p107.
48   A Gramsci, *Selections from Political Writings (1921-1926)*, op cit, p393.
49   Ibid, p333.

# Conclusion: then and now

1   E Francescangeli, op cit, p164. Although Bordiga and his followers were inveterate sectarians, in historical terms the PCI found itself facing a substantially new phenomenon – a mass movement of reaction. This is why some of the debate in the Communist movement assimilated fascism to older forms of reaction, such as the 'White Guards' in Russia. I owe this

observation to Ian Birchall.

2   M Rossi, op cit, p149.

3   R De Felice, *Mussolini il rivoluzionario 1883-1920* (Turin: Einaudi 1965), pp568, 589-590.

4   M Rossi, op cit, p150.

5   Ibid, p151.

6   *Times*, 1 November 1922.

7   Quoted ibid, 3 November 1922.

8   A Bernabei, *Esuli ed emigranti nel Regno Unito 1920-1940* (Milan: Mursia, 1997), p76.

9   R Bosworth, 'The British press, the Conservatives and Mussolini, 1920-1934', *Journal of Contemporary History* 5 (1970), p171.

10  Quoted in the *Times*, 3 November 1922.

11  Public Record Office: FO, 371/7660. Memo to Ronald Graham, British ambassador in Rome, 21 December 1922.

12  See C Levy, op cit, pp224-226. Antonio Gramsci probably would have been another fascist target, but he had been living in Moscow since May 1922.

13  Quoted in the *Times*, 21 January 1927.

14  *Times*, 5 October 1925.

15  F Carsten, op cit, p79.

16  A Hitler, *Mein Kampf* (Boston: Houghton Mifflin, 1971), p681.

17  E Francescangeli, op cit, p97.

18  T Behan, op cit, p37.

19  E Francescangeli, op cit, p144.

20  See T Behan, op cit; M Bianchi, 'A coloro che verranno', http://www.linea rossage.it/alberganti.htm

21  M Rossi, op cit, p100.

22  E Francescangeli, *Il Manifesto*, 4 August 2002. The official reason given, for what it is worth, is that Balbo was minister of aviation in the latter period of Mussolini's dictatorship.

23  C Bermani, op cit, pp181-187, 190-191.

24  *La Repubblica*, 26 July 2001.

25  Coordinamento Falcri Bnl, 'A futura memoria', in Aa.vv (eds), *Guerra civile globale*, op cit, p301.

26  Ibid, p329.

27  See C Bambery, 'Euro-Fascism: The Lessons of the Past and Current Tasks', *International Socialism* 60 (Autumn 1993), pp55-71, for an account of the transformation of European neo-fascism since 1945.

28  J Wolfreys, '"The Centre Cannot Hold": Fascism, the Left and the Crisis of French Politics', *International Socialism* 95 (Summer 2002), pp54-59.

29  *Il Manifesto*, 24 May 2002.

# Index

# The Resistible Rise of Benito Mussolini

Malatesta, Errico: 7, 32, 45, 48
Matteotti, Giacomo: 63, 96
Mazzini, Giuseppe: 5
Mussolini, Benito: 2-4, 18-20, 36,
39-40, 42-44, 46, 51, 53, 56, 63-
64, 66-67, 71, 73, 77, 85-87, 89-
90, 93-94, 96-97, 101, 108-114,
116, 119-120
as socialist: 11-12, 17

National Alliance (NA): 4, 117
Nenni, Pietro: 28, 87-88

*Ordine Nuovo* (*New Order*): 35-36,
41, 43-44, 61, 67, 69, 74, 92

Parma: 1-2, 15, 55-57, 77-87, 114-
116, 128n
PCI
birth: 37, 39, 44, 95
Communist squads: 50-51, 68, 81,
97-98
hostility to ADP: 2, 60, 67-69,
92-94, 106-108
membership: 44, 95, 114
relations with Moscow: 93-94, 96,
100-108
votes: 44
Picelli, Guido: 57, 78-87, 90, 114-
115
PSI
birth: 7-8
maximalists: 10, 26, 51
membership: 8, 25, 95, 114
'peace pact' with fascists
(August 1921): 62, 64-67, 70, 96
votes: 8-9, 11, 26, 44

Sarzana: 2, 63-64, 67, 70, 114
Secondari, Argo: 56-61, 69-70, 107,
115
Serrati, Giacinto: 18, 21, 30-31, 36,
65, 95-96, 100, 106
Socialist Party (see PSI)

Strikes
1896: 8
1904: 14-15
1914 and 'red week': 16, 19, 78,
122n
1915: 23
1919: 28, 31
1920: 29, 31-32, 94
'legalitarian' general strike
(August 1922): 49-51, 81
Syndicalism: 13-15, 18, 77-79

Tasca, Angelo: 35-36
Togliatti, Palmiro: 19, 35-36, 93
Trotsky, Leon: 36, 46, 60, 99-103,
105
Turati, Filippo: 7-9, 11-13, 20-21,
37, 40, 48, 65, 95-97, 100

United front: 4, 74, 80, 102-106,
108-109, 120
USI (anarchist union federation):
15, 25, 32, 35, 110

Zinoviev, Grigori: 94, 102-103